More praise for *Brand It Yourself*

"As a small business owner, I knew that branding was important, but I didn't know how to begin. *Brand It Yourself* is a fast-paced book with lots of concrete ideas to help me focus in on my branding message."

—Renee Duboff, president,
Personal Computer Training, Inc.

"This book captures the flexibility of Lynn's approach in addressing a range of concept development and branding challenges. Her method and billboard format is counterintuitive to our typical corporate process (as Lynn so nicely points out in her book), but after using it on six different projects, I can tell you, it works!"

—Molly Findley, product development
research fellow, Procter & Gamble

Brand It
YOURSELF

The Fast, Focused Way
to Marketplace Magic

LYNN ALTMAN

PORTFOLIO

PORTFOLIO
Published by the Penguin Group
Penguin Group (USA) Inc., 375 Hudson Street,
New York, New York 10014, U.S.A.
Penguin Group (Canada), 90 Eglinton Avenue East, Suite 700,
Toronto, Ontario, Canada M4P 2Y3
(a division of Pearson Penguin Canada Inc.)
Penguin Books Ltd, 80 Strand, London WC2R 0RL, England
Penguin Ireland, 25 St. Stephen's Green, Dublin 2, Ireland
(a division of Penguin Books Ltd)
Penguin Books Australia Ltd, 250 Camberwell Road, Camberwell,
Victoria 3124, Australia
(a division of Pearson Australia Group Pty Ltd)
Penguin Books India Pvt Ltd, 11 Community Centre, Panchsheel Park,
New Delhi – 110 017, India
Penguin Group (NZ), Cnr Airborne and Rosedale Roads, Albany,
Auckland 1310, New Zealand
(a division of Pearson New Zealand Ltd)
Penguin Books (South Africa) (Pty) Ltd, 24 Sturdee Avenue,
Rosebank, Johannesburg 2196, South Africa

Penguin Books Ltd, Registered Offices:
80 Strand, London WC2R 0RL, England

First published in 2006 by Portfolio,
a member of Penguin Group (USA) Inc.
Copyright © Lynn Altman, 2006
All rights reserved

Photograph credits appear on page 211.
Photos on pages 62, 156 and 158 courtesy of Jupiterimages
Photo of sponge monkeys on page 198 courtesy of Joel Veitch
Photo on page 102 courtesy of David Gabber / Photorazzi

LIBRARY OF CONGRESS CATALOGING IN PUBLICATION DATA

Altman, Lynn.
Brand it yourself: the fast, focused way to marketplace magic / Lynn Altman.
p. cm
Includes index.
ISBN 1-59184-106-2
1. Advertising—Brand name products.   2. Advertising—New products.   I. Title.
HF6161.B4A48 2006
659.1'11—dc22   2006050372

Printed in the United States of America
Set in Charter BT
Designed by Jaime Putorti
1   3   5   7   9   10   8   6   4   2

To April Thornton, our first client.
I always said that if I wrote a book
I would dedicate it to you.

Contents

Brand It
YOURSELF

Introduction

Over the past several years, branding has become the hot topic across corporate America—from large company conference rooms to the closet-size offices of small businesses. It has more recently evolved into a frenzied marketing race, with rule number one being: Get your product (or service) out there ahead of the competition, and get it quickly differentiated from the pack. It wasn't always this way. Years ago, branding was a slow, sometimes tedious process, a marathon dance with consumers that took forever. In today's world, however, the rules have changed. New products and brands seem to sprout instantly, some with a marketing campaign that take on an industry with the speed and agility of a hurricane. Red

Bull became a hit so quickly it must have made the marketing mavens at Coca-Cola and Pepsi insanely jealous. Is it always that simple, you're wondering. Yes . . . and no. Usually, there are some clever doings and hard work behind every fast-brand success story.

Branding continues to be a hot topic, and as with any hot topic, gurus arise. And they line up on all sides of the marketing spectrum. There are those doctrinaire experts who profess that creating a great brand takes months of consumer testing, endless insights, and millions in consumer learning and strategy before you can guarantee success. Others tell you that simple word association, blue-sky brainstorming, or insipid creative retreats will lead to Starbucks or iPod nirvana. Some gurus come equipped with pages of graphs, charts, and segmentation studies that will excuse them of any accountability should a new product fail. And naturally, there will always be those mavens who insist that the key to a client's branding needs rests solely and exclusively in the workings of his or her own genius mind. Old school, new wave, or any point in between, you'll find an expert, of course, for every point of view; and chances are, he or she already has weighed in on CNN's *Power Lunch*. What is at the heart of their pet philosophies and processes is this: Give me lots of time and gobs of money and a great brand will be invented. Occasionally it works, but, more often than not, it doesn't.

So what am I getting at? My basic notion is that too

many companies, too many marketing departments, and too many business owners spend too much time, too much angst, and far too much money on branding, especially when you consider the time constraints that today's marketers face. Winning the hearts and minds of the American consumer—or any consumer, for that matter—is not as daunting or pricey a task as you might initially think.

My partner and I founded our business on that belief, or rather the belief that what today's initiatives needed was creativity, simplicity, and intuition breathed into new product and branding efforts. We believed that there was a better, quicker, easier, and more efficient way to get the work done, and, perhaps most of all, that creating great brands is more art than science. When we first started the business, there was something revolutionary about what we were saying, and yet so sensible that meeting after meeting we would see clients nod their heads in subtle, subconscious agreement.

Starting in 1998, we ran full-page advertisements in the *New York Times*. We knew that most of the people we would actually work with were marketing directors and managers, but we also had a hunch that we had to generate interest in the upper executive levels of companies. Our theory was that the higher-ups would read our ad, love it, and then push it downward to the marketing manager as a "go get these guys to come in and let's see what they've got." The ad was always an all-text, no-nonsense explanation of who we were, what we did, and why. Year to year some copy elements would change, but the headline was always about this Branding or New Product Revolution that we were pioneering. The way we approach branding and new product invention is not what people call the Procter & Gamble way of thinking, and yet the package goods giant itself has called on us to help it develop multiple branding and new product initiatives. And that is a revolution indeed, not to mention a terrific endorsement.

We are not the typical gurus who charge $25,000 a day to dole out our particular brand of "exclusive" wisdom. In the following pages, I'm not going to express a pet philosophy, grind an ax, or give you a cute, New Age way to think about branding and new product creation. This book is a call to return to common sense and creativity.

And unlike other how-to books that have particular formulas that guarantee simple success, there is no secret, no science, no formula that can be plugged into a computer that can generate great brands and great ideas. What makes this book different is that I show you where to look for branding and new product ideas, but it is up to you to find them. What I've done is simplify an unnecessarily complicated process and put the tools for success in your hands.

Part of our process involves brainstorming workshops, where we put a hypothesis or potential opportunity on the table and stimulate responses that can turn into creative, effective brand solutions. I worded this carefully because I want to emphasize that I am never fully responsible for great brands that come out of our work. Often, it's the marketers and company employees who have the creative genius while I simply help elicit it. And that is the key to this thesis. My daily life is spent helping others come up with ideas, new products, and brands using a combination of client creativity and know-how with my particular expertise.

This book is designed to stimulate, motivate, and excite the creative lobe of your brain using the same kind of thinking and exercises that we use in our workshops. While not all hypotheses are the same for every project, there are some common ones, as well as ones that I can help you devise on your own.

If my job is to help companies create new products, brands, and initiatives, you're probably wondering, "Why can't these companies do it for themselves?"

It's a legitimate question, I admit, and one that has awakened me in the middle of the night in a cold sweat once or twice. Let's face it: If companies could do it for themselves, I'd be out of work in no time. Believe it or not, the quick response to the question is one that the companies already know. They're buried with too many projects, or they slip through the cracks ("the responsibility was on Bill's team, but Bill left the firm and the project is languishing"). There's a bureaucratic fear of acceptance (read "failure"), and this fear starts with the brand manager and sometimes runs all the way up the corporate food chain to the CEO's corner office. Other times, it's a long and dirty job, so nobody wants to do it, and finally somebody raises his hand at a meeting and says, "Let's just outsource it." Nobody argues with this logic. Send it to the very expensive hired guns. If they screw it up, we'll just bury the mistake. *Not our fault.*

Or take a look at another scenario: Bill's team has been working on the same brand for two years. They have attended countless hours of focus groups and pored over foot-high stacks of consumer research that has graphed, charted, pinpointed, circled, and zeroed in on every aspect of their core consumer needs, wants, fears, hopes, tastes, lifestyles, and perhaps favorite movies. Sometimes this research is useful. But unfortunately, it is not always insightful. Marketing departments can become so transfixed by their research that any kind of insight, intuition, or creative instinct is buried underneath the paperwork and cannot find a way out.

So whether it's paralysis from analysis or blame-free management in action, these scenarios occur all the time and help explain why there's a certain amount of inertia when it comes to brand innovation in corporate America.

And as they insist, it's not their fault. Yes, there are minions of smart people working within the walls of these companies, but the reporting and approval structure ("let's be careful, folks, we can't mess this one up") is designed to slow them down to a crawl. Or sabotage them completely. It's hard to get a new concept out the door in six years, let alone six months. By playing it safe with plain ideas that will placate the boss, the creative factor in the equation is either reduced or eliminated. It's a disease you could call creative inertia.

And consumers are no better at change than anyone else. Why is the favorite flavor of everything either pizza or cheese? In the stock market, it is assumed that stockholders have a certain amount of power and consumers are the stockholders of new products and brands. If they don't want something different and if they reject it in any kind of testing, their veto power is beyond question. Few companies are brave enough to create the kind of buzz that inspires instead of placates, that tells consumers what they want instead of asking them.

Beyond the superficial explanations, however, looms the real answer to the question, "Why can't the companies do it themselves?"

People sometimes forget how to think creatively. Everyone at some point in his or her life has had an "I could have had a V8 moment" (a truly simple, but brilliant, idea). This is when, upon seeing the solution, you cannot believe that you didn't see it sooner. The solutions that I help people come up with almost always evolve from an idea that, if it wasn't under their nose, was at least in the proximity of their face. In the following pages, I'm going to quantify the creative process as it relates to branding and show you how to put your own brainpower to work in coming up with new concepts for your company or your clients.

Some consultants and "think-tank" facilitators use all sorts of gimmicks and tactics to stimulate creativity. From the Eureka Mansion, where executives pay upward of $150,000 to spend three days going barefoot and hitting each other with Nerf balls, to self-proclaimed guru Faith Popcorn, whose outrageous hair and New Age "clicking" simply plays into the mystique that ideas are a very scarce, expensive commodity. The underlying theme is that it requires someone "really out there" in order to sculpt those ideas into commercial concepts. Most of Faith Popcorn's output comes straight from the pages of popular magazines. Her staff scours them, and she synthesizes and distills them into "trends." Her clients actually find some of her work useful. But it just proves that thinking creatively can become a very expensive exercise if you allow it to.

But who am I and what makes me so different from these other experts that I feel so quick to brand as false idols? I think one of the key differences—if not *the* key difference—is that my goal is to empower others to recognize and recharge their own creative resources and not to blow their marketing budget on snake oil solutions. Our down-to-earth, straightforward sensibility—and my sense of consultant-related righteousness—can be traced to my professional origins.

My partner, Joe Viverito, and I met as subcontractors for a midsize consulting firm on a project for a large packaged goods company.

Joe and I were hired hands whose job it was to write multiple concept statements that would be used in market research for one of those consultants entrenched in the belief that they have to test concepts with the words "Such and such makes me feel happy because it enhances my life," or "Such and such makes me feel confident because I can count on this product." Joe and I knew that trying to get consumers to react to these dry, skull-crushingly boring, and meaningless statements was not really getting to the heart and soul of what great brands are supposed to be about.

The consultants we worked for would take these "insight-driven" statements and show them to consumers in a focus group setting so that they could react to the different statements. And somehow, from this research, clients were going to create a wonderful brand that was full of life, excitement, and motivation that would make it impossible for consumers to resist.

We couldn't help but think, "What's wrong with this picture?" The answer was that so much was wrong with that picture we didn't know where to start. First, with consultants and agencies hiring so many subcontractors and freelancers, projects became victims of the old telephone-game routine. A message or idea would pass through so many hands that its original intention was often lost in the static. Also, because of all of the jobs going on at one time, each project took seemingly forever. Progress was slow, choppy, and belabored, and each project was competing against another for attention. Meanwhile, team members came and went, energy levels sank, and objectives got reprioritized constantly—mostly as a result of boredom and overthink.

What usually came out of these branding exercises, if you can call them that, were concept statements or positioning statements that were shown to consumers in focus groups or in quantitative testing. Call us crazy, but it struck us as very wrong that consumers were expected to react to long, overdrawn, emotion-free statements that typically included some kind of generalized picture, often drawn in line art. If the product was for a kitchen cleaner, there would be a three-inch picture of a woman in a kitchen paired with twenty lines of copy touching on every benefit of the cleaner, and yes, including the kitchen sink. We couldn't help but wonder how consumers were supposed to differentiate strategic propositions that maybe had one word changed in each concept. The word "easy" was replaced with "fast" in one concept and then with "simple" in another. Most of the time, the concepts talked so much about what the product did, that it totally neglected the consumers and their interaction with the product.

Where were the emotions and the instant connections that people feel in marketplace reality? Where was the sizzle and the attitude, like the kind that forced people to "think different" about Apple computers? If consumers were shown a concept statement for Apple in the way they are for kitchen cleaners, it would say something along the lines of: "This computer is the one brand of computer that is user friendly [or cute or alternative or modern or fill in any other word here]."

We weren't surprised when a client's market research came out flat because consumers did not react at all differently from one concept to the next. Nowhere in these long and laborious research models and strategic statements could we find the marketplace magic that consumers truly respond to. And although this may sound rude, Joe and I couldn't help but wonder why clients were looking to focus group participants to create brands. Wasn't that their job?

These projects I worked on seemed unnecessarily unproductive and I couldn't help but dream about how I could do it better. Luckily, Joe felt the same, and soon after meeting on a few freelance gigs we began to crack the branding code.

The first part, undoubtedly, was timing. If we did it our way, we would only work on one project at a time and not pass work along to juniors or freelancers. Then, we thought, we would create ideas that were both emotional and strategic—ideas that gave both consumers and marketers something resembling marketing reality. So many ideas, we found, never really got off the ground until that essential marketplace magic was in place. How could Charmin have owned "softness" without creating its "squeezability"? We wanted to create this kind of personality, persuasion, and legacy that are at the heart of successful brands. That's why we decided to craft our ideas into true-to-life introductory advertisements, not sterile, muddy concept statements. We wanted the discipline and the inventiveness that comes with the challenge of actually *selling* the concept (without actually being in the ad business). Lastly, Joe and I decided, if we were to do it our way, we wouldn't be greedy. We would give clients a range of meaningful ideas fairly quickly for a reasonable fee. What we couldn't foresee at the time was that we had stumbled upon many creative disciplines that have led to the incredible success of our fast-track branding methodology.

My techniques, honed over years of experience, center

around our Brandmaker Express process, which flies in the face of both traditional branding companies and greedy gurus alike. Joe and I created this process in response to all the pseudomystique and needless jargon that hung around branding like parasitic groupies. In the following pages, I will show you how our firm has taken on some of the largest and most successful brands in the world and turned their marketing departments, managers, and CMOs into fast-track believers.

To date, fifty-four of the Top 100 Global Brands and Brand Portfolios have used our process for their branding and new product efforts, including: Coca-Cola, Microsoft, Gillette, McDonald's, Marlboro, American Express, Pepsi, Merrill Lynch, Morgan Stanley, Nestlé, Kellogg's, Panasonic, Smirnoff, Pizza Hut, UBS, L'Oréal, Colgate, Johnson & Johnson, Kodak, and Wendy's. Add to that some of our favorite clients, including Procter & Gamble, General Mills, Capital One, and Church & Dwight, who have honored us with incredible repeat business across many of their business units and brands.

We have used our unique ten-day process in more than three hundred instances to help some of the world's best-known companies create ideas for new products, new services, new brands, and new ad campaigns. You will learn how to use the creative disciplines of the process in order to attack and conquer any branding need. I will teach you how to, in fact, brand it yourself.

Our Not-So-Secret Recipe for Branding Success

In order to be successful, you must first appear so.

—*François de la Rochefoucauld*

The second hardest thing Joe and I ever did was to create our unique business model. The hardest was getting a client to actually give it a try. Equipped with a phone and a fax machine (e-mail had not yet reached full force), we bought a list of contacts from a local focus group facility and did what any new business owners must do—made cold calls. The voice mails of countless executives were filled with our pitch about how we could create great new products and brands in just ten days. For anyone who has done this kind of phone work, it is heartless at best.

Normally, it's just plain cruel because the rejection rate is so high. But we knew that in order to test our model, we had to get the business; and so we simply made the calls.

Not a whole lot of excitement those first few months. A big day for us was getting an actual meeting. We'd don our suits and come equipped with our rudimentary new business presentation that included some laminates to go for an overhead projector and a few products that Joe and I had actually worked on as freelancers in the past. This was a tricky tightrope between good salesmanship and false advertising. But we knew from early on that no client would want to be the guinea pig, so we had to talk about our business as if it had been going on for years.

During one particularly fateful business meeting, our biggest hopes and worst fears occurred simultaneously— the client gave us a job. Our first (unbeknownst to them) official project was with Pepsi-Cola. A few weeks after that, we landed our second client: Merrill Lynch. And soon after that, Lipton would be the third. ("But can't you get any big clients?" I remember my father teasing.) My own disbelief at what was happening was overshadowed by the recognition that we really might be on to something revolutionary. When we created the Brandmaker Express, our business model and concept was founded on three key notions: speed, output, and cost. Working quickly made for better focus; giving clients concepts that resembled introductory ads was a more realistic way to create and convey marketplace magic; and the friendly fee made us an extremely low-risk option. What I don't think we realized was the simple wisdom of what we had created.

Our simple wisdom can be distilled as follows:

1. Timing Is Everything
2. Count to One
3. Keep It Simple

How to Avoid "Overthinking"

When we were subcontracting for other consultants and agencies, we were astounded at the amount of time that projects would take. Simply developing an idea required a flock of focus groups, rounds of revisions, and mountains of market research. When the market research departments of the corporate world are through probing the consciousness of the American consumer, they end up with so much information it might make a CIA spook blush. And therein lies the problem: At the end of the stack of paperwork and the reams of data is a lot of confusion and little direction. Add in the other casualties of time such as clients moving jobs, bureaucracy, people second-guessing their own ideas, and too many decision makers with different pet objectives and—voilà!—you've now got a classic case of corporate project inertia.

The other curse of long-term projects reads like a corollary of Parkinson's Law: The time it takes to do anything expands exponentially with the amount of time you allow yourself to do it. And, the more time we've invested to reach a certain goal, the more importance it takes on, and the more dependent we become on its success. No one wants to abandon a sinking ship, especially one that took nearly a year to build. What happens, then, is that people start seeing only what they want to see and then use research to justify their actions.

Oscar Wilde probably put it best when he said, "Time is a waste of money." Time is indeed a strange resource, at various times worth more than anything or next to nothing. Everyone has had the feeling that given enough time, he or she can do a very good job on a given task or project. Time can have a strange, counterintuitive effect on the creative mind, however. Having lots of time is important if you're contemplating the origins of the universe, but it can be a detriment if you're trying to come up with a new marketing concept for a product that's set to launch during the upcoming holiday selling season. Instead of repeating the often heard lament, "If I only had more time . . ." try rephrasing it to, "It's a good thing we don't have that much time."

Time really takes its toll on discipline, energy, and focus. Often, clients and consultants get so accustomed to their own ideas that they start tinkering with them because they no longer seem new; adding new twists and turns that confuse and distract from the initial branding imperative. Here's an example to illustrate my point: Have you noticed if you get ready to leave the house and you have ten minutes to spare, you start fiddling—with your hair, your clothes, your shoes, and suddenly you're running around trying to fix everything that ten minutes ago you were feeling pretty good about? That's what I call overthinking or mental fidgeting. Too much of that can ruin even the most promising idea.

Or how about this: You know you have a week or a month to complete a project so you wait until the last minute. Either that, or you'll peck away at it in between others that carry a more pressing deadline. Of course, conflicting obligations and busy lifestyles require us to work that way. But just because it's ubiquitous doesn't mean it's efficient or effective.

Just Do It . . . Faster

There's an easy way to avoid creative ruts and traps—do it quicker. Speed gives you focus, energy, and prevents common snafus that arise from having very broad or loosely defined deadlines. The worst thing you can hear from a client is, "We're not in a hurry. Get it to us when you can." If it's not their priority, it's certainly not going to be yours, especially when your own calendar gets increasingly busier.

Proceeding with dispatch forces you to think differently about time management. For me, it means working on one project at a time and knowing exactly how much time I need to allow for each step of the process. That way, I don't have to drop dead in order to reach a certain deadline because I know exactly when each deadline is (ten days away, to be exact). This allows me to relax and truly dedicate my entire focus to whichever assignment is the current one. Ten days also gives me some comfort in knowing that whatever I'm working is not going to last forever.

Therefore, when you refocus your time and set rigid time limits, you'll see increased productivity and enthusiasm for your project. With speed also comes a sense of completion and productivity, and—guess what?—at the end of that assignment, you'll be primed to begin your next mission.

Count to One (and Then Stop)

Knowing that my goal at the end of the ten days is somewhere between eighteen and twenty separate and distinct branding options, I start by looking in separate and distinct opportunity areas. That's why the first exercise I do with any project is to break it into manageable parts. Companies have an ingrained bad habit of wanting to extol every great feature and benefit of their product instead of examining how each one individually can hold the secret to creating the best branding message. In my experience, this could be their single most common misunderstanding of the marketplace. There's a reason why there are no face creams that simultaneously repair, renew, cleanse, soften, exfoliate, and deliver younger-looking skin. Conversely, we don't buy a shampoo that doubles as a face wash and hand soap. Cosmetic companies learned long ago that with multiplicity comes perceived inefficacy. In our age of advanced specialization (branding expert being one such example), it should come as no surprise that we believe that certain brands and certain products do their best at performing specific tasks. Part of thinking single-mindedly is not only musing about what a product or service does, but how the target audience interacts with it—emotionally, physically, or otherwise.

A friend, an account planner in an ad agency, told me about some work she was doing with Advil. At the time, Aleve had really begun to take market share with their long-lasting and perceived higher efficacy claims, which used to be Advil's claim. This, coupled with the rise of countless generic brands of ibuprofen, caused Advil to lose its leadership edge. After lots of consumer research, the two (not one!) points that emerged as most important to consumers were "strength of relief" and "speed of relief."

No surprise there. But instead of choosing one, the client decided that since both points were equally important to consumers, they would flaunt them equally. Remember the campaign? "Fast. Strong. Advil." Of course you don't. Neither does anyone else. Care to guess why? It was such a nonmessage to consumers because in trying to stand for two things, it ended up standing for neither. It got even worse: With Aleve owning strength and Tylenol going for trust, Advil added one more word to their tagline, so it read: Fast. Strong. Trusted.

I ran into similar difficulties with bathroom tissue. I was trying to position a premium Quilted Northern bathroom-tissue paper based on a new and exciting technology. At the time, they had second place in market share after Charmin. The research indicated that the two things that consumers wanted most from their bathroom tissue were softness and freshness, and unfortunately, Charmin spent millions to lay claim to softness. That left our brand the pretty bleak claim to freshness. Do you know anyone who buys toilet paper because it's fresh? Or better yet, do you know anyone who rejects a certain toilet paper brand because it's not fresh?

Interestingly, no matter what technology or material Quilted Northern would tout, it simply could not trump Charmin, the master of softness. It's a great reminder about how important it is to stand for one thing and own it, even if it's something that other companies could say about their product. It also teaches another lesson: Don't try to fight a branding battle you have little chance of winning.

Sometimes it's scary to commit to being just one thing to one specific group of people. It seems counterintuitive and overly risky. Clients fear that consumers won't understand how truly amazing their product is because they won't understand the vast amount of wonderful things the product can do. But the sacrifice is well worth it when it comes to conveying—and trading on—a meaningful message. The one exception to this theory is if your client is Swiss Army knife and your key attribute is being able to do lots of things at once. But even in that case their "one" thing is that a Swiss Army knife does everything. If you're not Swiss Army knife, then remember: There is infinite marketplace wisdom in owning one specific thing, whether it is something emotional, functional, image-based, or otherwise. Somewhere this rings true deep down inside every smart marketer. Yet too many companies and too many marketers can't learn the lesson that trying to be everything to everyone amounts to being nothing to no one. Our process allows us to say everything, but to say it one message at a time. In that way, we can see which message is the strongest without feeling like we left any option unexplored.

When Joe worked in advertising, he had the great fortune of working under Rosser Reeves, the acknowledged king of the Unique Selling Proposition, or USP. Notice that this term is singular, not plural. So it makes sense that in trying to discover the USP, we first have to find the U. Over the past ten years, we have become very experienced and adept at finding ways to uncover that USP. Where lots of consultants and agencies like to immediately put things in proverbial "buckets," what we're trying to do is to overturn those buckets and examine the contents inside. The gold nugget is usually there, but it's hidden underneath the silt in the river, and I may have to sift through a lot of gravel and sand to find it. It's not that I know what I'll find, rather that over the years I've honed my skills of knowing where to look, which is what I'll share with you.

Keep It Simple—Really Simple

We all know that any joke you have to explain is probably not worth telling. Same thing when it comes to creating a great brand or new product. Of course, there are plenty of consultants and marketing types out there who will say that within any concept statement, there is an imperative to have a key insight, a core consumer benefit, plus a compelling reason to believe, and have it all neatly explained for the consumer. But if you've got to do that much explaining to tell your consumer why they want what you're offering, then you're probably in serious trouble. When you are creating a poster, a billboard, even a package, you are never going to have the luxury of explaining all of those things to your audience.

Consumers are just not going to read the manual, literally or figuratively. It has to be intuitive, and it has to be in a flash. Same thing goes for many of the most important vehicles for conveying a branding message, including logos, packaging, direct mail, or even a few words that are going to fit on the back of your business card. These are the key elements of communication and these are the ones you want to make sure get communicated as clearly and concisely as possible.

I've always believed that it was important to bring our ideas to a finished marketplace look and feel, but what the process hit upon was the incredible role that simplicity plays in all of this. Our creative medium is the print advertisement, and it's never been because we were itching to get our ideas into your favorite magazine. Not only did the print ad discipline force us to approach ideas single-mindedly, it also became a disciplined method for filtering out the more complex and harder-to-convey ideas. In print your meaning has to come across quickly; your message has to go right from the page into the psyche of whomever you're trying to sell to. You can't rely on cute situations or fancy camera work of the TV spot that agencies have come to worship. Conversely, you avoid the swamp of strategic statements ("This product is for healthy-minded, early adopters who are fashion enthusiasts and highly evolved when it comes to purchasing lip liner") meaningful only to marketers and their kind.

A Homemade Recipe for Success

Ironically, we didn't know we had hit upon the winning combination of fast-track Branding at the inception of our business. It was only after doing a few dozen projects that we realized what we had: Speed and timing were an original part of our ten-day model, where we found again and again that the right kind of focus and energy was essential to producing fresh concepts full of excitement; single-mindedness came out of the way that we began to search for ideas by dissecting project objectives and product attributes, using very specific thought-starters in our workshops in order to confront the challenges that came our way; simplicity showed its importance when we were developing and creating our finished output as we saw how it forced the best ideas to rise to the top.

What was more exciting than how important each aspect was to the success of each project, was to see how well these parts work together. Speed, simplicity, single-mindedness. Attack any challenge, take it apart, develop the most promising ideas, communicate them clearly, repeat as desired.

The way that these three elements all work together

gives our team an incredible amount of energy and passion for each project and the output itself demands that the best ideas emerge. Whenever we're stuck, we go back to the basics, just as any professional does in any endeavor.

We also have the great fortune of starting anew every ten days, so we go from credit cards to toothbrushes to snack foods to household cleaners and then back to the financial services world, all within a few months. And as you'll soon see, the skills you'll need to develop are easily transferable to any category.

2 The Recipe in Action

The recipe for success is only as good as the cake it bakes. So while you might agree (or not) with the theories behind our business model, you're probably wondering how it actually works to solve any number of branding and new product needs. By understanding what I go through on a day-to-day, project-to-project, challenge-to-challenge basis, you will better see how you can learn to become an expert brander in the chapters to come.

The Brandmaker Express process all starts with a thorough briefing. In most cases, this is a two-hour, face-to-face meeting where the client tells me his challenge, wishes, and objectives. This can range anywhere from a very broad new product assignment, such as: "What's the next new line of cough and cold products?" to a very specific repositioning effort with a very specific audience, such as "create a meaningful repositioning communication for Wheaties cereal targeted to the boomer market." The range of assignments—and products—that I encounter is truly amazing. One week I'm branding a new small business loan, the next week I'm creating the latest greatest finger food for four-year-olds. But no matter what the assignment, there are two essential questions that I must be able to answer before I feel comfortable moving on. The first is, "What are the client's goals and best wishes for the product?" Lots of times, clients have multiple audiences, multiple objectives, or they have a larger plan that my project is just a small part of. Other times there are certain "buckets" (marketing-speak for areas) they want me to work within or imperatives that each concept must meet. By understanding what the real expectations are for the project output, I can do a much better job of meeting them. Disappointment is one of the worst emotions you can ever evoke from a client, and death of the business to boot. But such disenchantment can come from being *too* creative, not just the other way around.

That brings me to the other "must-have" of a briefing: As important as knowing client *wants* is knowing client *won'ts*. I am ever surprised at the number of consultants and gurus who shove their pet philosophies and their own favorite ideas down a client's product pipeline. Why would I ever want to create new products or branding options that could not or would not stand a chance when there are plenty of ideas that will? There's no point in having a brilliant idea if it's totally unusable, which is exactly what makes this kind of creativity so challenging and rewarding. For an idea to be a good one, it has to also provide a workable solution.

The balance of setting expectations and limitations—in my work as well as yours—is essential to success. Before you do anything, you should be able to articulate—to yourself if no one else—exactly what you are hoping to achieve in your branding endeavor. How do you find this out? Ask questions.

While there are certain questions that are common to all briefings, such as target audience and competition, there is no formal guideline to what questions I ask. In most cases, a briefing is a cross between a brain dump and a therapy session, where every bit of information I get leads me to a question that might dig deeper into the psyche of the audience, manufacturer, or product itself. If a financial company told me they want to brand a credit card for busy people, I might ask what these people are busy doing or what they wish they had more time to do instead of thinking about credit cards. Or if the product is a line of hair care products geared toward twenty-one-year-old women who love washing, conditioning, and styling their hair, I might ask what they like about it or how they feel once they're through with their coiffing routine.

Sometimes, the briefing is no more than a conversation, other times the client has outlined every last detail, fact, figure, table, and graph based on weeks or months— even years—of market research. Neither way is better than the other. I love information in all its forms and would like to think that I pull out what I need from either one of those scenarios.

Each new assignment gives my brain a real creative buzz. That's because my mind is simultaneously swimming in a pool of possibilities while trying to wrap itself around the complexities that each project brings. I get a rush of energy (and sometimes fear) and I don't want to wait too long to get my thoughts down on paper.

Have you ever left a meeting totally jazzed about what was being discussed and had so many ideas you couldn't wait to start? What happened to those ideas? Most of the time, they get diminished by other tasks and responsibilities and fall into the wasteland of "good meetings that went nowhere." That's why immediately following the briefing and before the excitement subsides, I'm writing down all the possible ways to solve the challenge at hand. These include, but aren't limited to, identifying specific functional, emotional, visual, and tactical opportunities. I also write down, in very broad strokes, the areas I think might be fertile ground. In some cases, it can be a word or a phrase, a characteristic, an attitude, or a general style I find promising even if I can't quite visualize how it's going to play out. In other cases, I instantly imagine a solution but have to find the creative meat that will make it a strong piece of communication. Just like waking up in the middle of a night from a dream that I swear I'll remember in the morning and then don't, writing my initial ideas down is an invaluable discipline for me. I know that I can come back to these notes later, discard some, add others— but if I wait a few days I'll never be able to recapture those first sparks of creative thought.

The next step in the process is translating each opportunity area into an exercise for two invention workshops that take place a few days after the briefing. Unlike a lot of blue-sky brainstorming sessions, these workshops are highly disciplined and designed to elicit potential solutions for one specific hypothesis at a time. In a typical branding project, I'm looking for these solutions in the form of names, headlines, taglines, rally cries, and photographic images. Again, not because I am an advertising wannabe, but because these mediums give me an abbreviated, marketplace-driven communication for a certain brand or idea. I also want to fashion the exercises to force people to express themselves in ways they've never had to before. For example, if I think the key to certain brand communication is the fact that it's "easy to use," I might ask how Calvin Klein, in his one-word simplicity, would name an easy-to-use product. Or I might ask for a song title or lyric that already has the word or thought of "easy" in it, such as "Easy Rider," "ABC, Easy as One Two Three" or "Take It Easy." (It's interesting to note that one of the most creative challenges of the process is developing the format for the workshops. The format is my version of trend analysis, my strategy sheet, my marketing plan; and it is the step that is most responsible for carving out new creative opportunities and solutions.) The benefit from creating the format is twofold: As much as it helps me get a grasp on the project, the parameters, and its possibilities, the exercises themselves are responsible for generating an incredible amount of raw creative material—bits, pieces, and parts of ideas that will act as creative inspiration and fodder for our finished concepts.

In the end, there are about thirty exercises that comprise the format for the workshops. A team of two facilitates the session tag-team style, so that with each exercise comes a fresh voice and a fresh face. No one ever has more than thirty seconds to respond to an exercise because—especially in a brainstorming environment—I want only their initial responses, which are as instinctive as they are intuitive. Those top-of-mind replies are the ones that generate the best ideas, the best products, and the best brands precisely because that's how consumers shop—intuitively, instinctively, impulsively—and the more of those cues I can tap into, the better.

There are two consecutive workshops per project. The first includes a range of participants from the client side, including the tried and true folks in marketing, sales, market research, and product development. But we also love having the less-than-predictable participants from legal, finance, and operations. They have the knowledge of the product or brand, without having the common "been there, done that" mentality that lots of the marketing veterans have. The added bonus to having a diversified group is that everyone gets excited when they start to see the possibilities at hand, and also feel (and rightfully so) that they played a role in its success.

The second workshop taps into the creative minds of people whom we call our Creative Souls. These are entrepreneurial and inventive people who, by vocation or avocation, are creating the trends and not following them. These creative souls come from the fashion industry, the cosmetics industry, graphic design, editors and contributors to popular magazines, creative writers, actors, bartenders, chefs—there may even be an extremely creative marketing maven in the mix. They are incredibly inventive, expressive, use none of the typical jargon, remain blissfully unaware of internal buzzwords, and have complete freedom from the negative baggage that the client may have accumulated. Now be very sure that this is not a focus group, nor is it intended to be. The clients have already covered the close-in thinking, based on experience, knowledge, and familiarity with the objectives at hand. And because the format is so specific and disciplined, these fresh minds only react to what we give them, which ensures that even if they don't know a lot about a particular subject, they can still create ideas relevant to the project. Some more traditional marketers might find this hard to believe, but I've seen it happen again and again.

The key client team is there to observe this second creative workshop. The team has already participated the previous day, so this gives it a chance to be a little more subjective. The team members can listen to the actual strategies and thinking behind each exercise in the format, and also take a step back and listen to the responses that spout from the mouths of this very dynamic, creative group. Some of the ideas that come out of the second workshop reiterate and substantiate the client responses, which is good. To me that means that people who have rarely—if ever—thought about this particular business react and respond in the same way as those who think about it all the time. Other answers, to be sure, are totally new and different than anything any of us have heard or thought of up until that point. Admittedly, half of it is what Joe likes to call "dreck," which means that it's either too weird, too already done in the category, or just too . . .

too. But the other half, well it's a mother lode of raw material and nuggets of genius that add greatly to our work and our output.

Immediately following the second workshop, we meet with our clients for what we call the Reality Check Luncheon. This is where the single-minded thinking really comes into play. After two very intensive invention days, I've been exposed to lots and lots of ideas. My job now is to pick out what I feel are the areas worth pursuing. How do I do that? How do I know which ideas are worthy and which are not? The "I know it when I see it" method of Justice Potter Stewart is the methodology I practice. Certain areas of exploration are more fruitful, and it's obvious from both the quantity and quality of the replies for that particular exercise. Other words or visual thoughts make every person nod his or her head and make each of us wish that we had been the one to create it. These are the good ideas and they naturally rise to the top.

I start the discussion with about thirty to thirty-five of the ideas I find most promising and review each single-minded area with the client. I am looking for their thumbs-up, thumbs-down, cautionary words, or red flags for each conceptual area. Together, we usually narrow the list down to a workable twenty potential areas for creative development. This reality check is not a frivolous step by any means. I know that my team has only ten working days to create twenty fully developed concepts, and I have no interest in wasting valuable time or effort on any less-than-favorite solution areas. This is such an essential step in our success because it allows us to communicate on a very practical and tactical level with our clients. There's no blue sky, no pontificating, no fancy words (like pontificating)—just the cut-to-the-chase identifying of the areas to move ahead with and a comfort level for everyone involved. I know that I can continue developing the ideas that are prestamped for approval and the client knows that the only surprises will be how the concepts come to life.

The ten-day countdown begins here. It marks the time from concept agreement to creative execution of the ideas and is crucial to achieving marketplace magic. Any consultant can paper the walls with a million ideas but few actually see them through to a finished product or brand. The discipline of bringing the ideas to finished form lets us and our clients see what happens when the theoretical and the strategic become real. The ideas are flung from the safety of research-friendly concept statements, theoretical products, and branding strategies and brought into the uncertain world of consumer communications. They will become vulnerable to all the same irrationalities, ideosyncracies, and impulses that real products and brands must face.

All of the work I do is presented in the form of an introductory print advertisement. Again, not because my secret hope is to break into the advertising world, but because the print medium forces ideas to be communicated quickly and concisely without the luxury of a hundred-word concept statement or a thirty-second television spot. During this step, my partners and I literally tackle each concept one at a time. We create headlines, taglines, and visual thoughts first, since those are the three key touch points of our style of communication. We start out by focusing in on what we want to say and see if any of the verbatims from the workshops or ones we create on our own could work. Sometimes it's a name or a visual that gives us the key to communicating the idea. In any case, we know that each idea has to be easy to understand, compelling, and singular in focus. This requires a lot of pushing, pulling, and refining in order for it to work.

Here is what you might overhear, if you were a fly on our office wall:

Lynn: Let's do the concept about consumer satisfaction.

Joe: Okay. Someone at the workshop had that line, "Your customers will be satisfied for a lifetime."

Lynn: Well, that also has longevity in it. I think we should just focus on satisfaction, something like: "Satisfy your soul."

Joe: That doesn't really make sense to me. Is there something visually we can do that says satisfaction?

> Lynn: How about just a close-up of a smile, like a billboard, with the words: "You are here."
>
> Joe: Love it! Then the enduring rally cry can be: "Get satisfied here."

It's an odd example, I admit, because it's totally out of context and without a real product in mind. However, there are a few interesting things going on in this kind of interaction, which is the point of the example in the first place. First of all, it's a constant discipline to come up with a truly single-minded idea. Secondly, ideas do not happen all at once—it's good to have someone to bounce ideas off of if possible, and, if you don't, then it's good to play devil's advocate with yourself. Create ideas in a vacuum and you usually come up with clouds of dust. Lastly, and perhaps most important, there's a huge difference between a strategic direction such as "satisfaction" and the consumer-friendly expression of what that actually means.

There's a second scenario here and one that I think bears mentioning. This is when the idea sounds good on paper, but is very difficult to bring to life in a concept. It typically happens when an idea is too broad, too convoluted, or trying to do too many things at one time. Often, we don't know it is any of those things until the actual moment we try to convert it into consumer-focused language and visuals. Take a look at scenario B, this time with a product:

Lynn: Let's take a swing at "customer satisfaction because of our one-page approach to insurance."

Joe: Okay. How about, "One page and you'll be happy."

Lynn: One page of what? How about, "After just one page, our customers are happy."

Joe: No . . . it doesn't really say enough about what the one page is all about. How about if we give the one page a more formalized name, like: "We're proud to introduce the One-Page Approach to insurance."

Lynn: I love that idea, but now it's missing customer satisfaction. But at least now I get what the idea is all about.

In a case like that, we may decide that since we've covered customer satisfaction in another concept, the real news here is indeed this unique one-page approach. Maybe customer satisfaction becomes more of an umbrella concept for lots of different product thoughts, such as the one-pager. Point is, a lot of times, consultants who stay in the theoretical don't have to put their ideas through the same kind of practical filter, and never get to see exactly how message hierarchies can work within a brand. Conversely, if we only thought executionally without having to commit to one specific selling message, then we'd be no better than ad agencies who often fall victim to very creative—however hollow—communication.

The process of bringing the ideas to life in this one-at-a-time fashion takes nearly three full days. For each one, we have to agree on a thematic set of words as well as a visual thought that best conveys every single concept. We have to be able to envision how it might play out, and also make sure that each one could potentially provide a real and complete solution to the challenge at hand. And when twenty concepts are at stake, it amounts to a lot of work. When naming is involved, it typically happens during this time, although names are tough and can slow down the project momentum, so we often add in names throughout the ten days. Once we have the headlines, taglines, and potential names with the ideal visuals in mind, we meet with our art directors who are responsible for understanding what each concept is about and finding the right kind of images and pictures that will best communicate each idea. We don't want to show a general, meaningless picture of a woman smiling in her kitchen simply because we're talking about a dishwashing product. If the idea about this dish soap is that it will take less time to wash the dishes, then we want to show the woman specifically leaving the kitchen, not standing in it. As the art directors search image banks, stock photography sources, and magazines for the right kind of pictures, it again forces us to make sure that the ideas we have envisioned can actually be communicated. Sometimes the art directors tell us that our ideas don't make enough sense, sometimes they find a picture and we realize that it's the picture we want, but the words we initially chose have to be revised. Other times (and I truly love when this happens), they find a picture, and it either changes our thinking altogether or inspires a whole new concept we had never thought about before. And thanks to so many online resources such as Google Images and royalty-free stock photography sites, it shouldn't be hard for you to also find the pictures that best suit your concept.

Once the pictures are in place and the ideas are beginning to take form, we return to the concept wording. For each concept we must write a concise paragraph of supporting copy that explains in very brief terms exactly what the concept is about and the reasons to believe whatever it is that we're asserting in each one. I am a staunch believer in the three sentence rule: Say what the concept is about, why the product fulfills that idea, and say "see you later" with a nice wrap-up thought. To continue with the dishwashing liquid concept, we might say:

> *Speed up your dishwashing routine with **One & Done** dishwashing liquid. This incredible dishwashing treatment contains fast-acting beads that go to work fast and rinse off in a flash. Plus, it comes in such great scents and is so gentle on your hands, you'll fall in love in an instant.*

Considering that this short paragraph is still three sentences more than consumers ever read about a certain product, there is a definite takeaway here, which is speeding up your dishwashing routine. There have been projects where we've taken much more of the billboard approach, where the visual element and main headline told the entire story and body copy simply didn't exist. This happens more often with high imagery brands, such as spirits, fashion, and other nonfunctional categories where clients knew there would never be an actual "reason to believe" in the product's communication. Take Absolut vodka as an example. The imagery *was* the brand. If forced into a typical marketing-concept writing, it would say something absurd such as "Absolut vodka is the brand you drink when you want to reflect your sophisticated self" or "The more you drink Absolut vodka the better you will feel about yourself."

All of this creative development takes us ten full days. On day eleven, we're back to our clients with the finished project, and they're typically quite delighted. Sometimes they have minor refinements with a visual choice, name, or product claim. Other times, they go straight from presentation to research, utilizing the concepts in qualitative or online testing.

I know you must be wondering about the times when a presentation has failed. Thankfully, there have not been that many, but they do happen and usually one or more of the following four elements are in play: The key decision maker has not been present throughout the process and doesn't see his or her pet idea in the mix; there are multiple agencies working on the same project and competition (and criticism) becomes fierce; objectives are elusive and change several times throughout the project; or, we screwed up. While the built-in reality checks and spectrum of ideas lessen the likelihood of a total train wreck, snafus are unavoidable. I remember right before one presentation the client was mad because he had wanted us to join him for lunch but we couldn't because we had to catch the last plane out in order to get to a meeting in another city the following morning. In our defense, no one mentioned anything about lunch, but that was not taken into account. He sent down his subordinate to tell us that he "was not a happy man" and that we had to change our travel arrangements, which we couldn't. So we presented to an already unhappy client who had some other agencies at the presentation who took advantage of our doghouse status and critiqued nearly every concept we presented. Years later, this client switched companies and hired us on four separate accounts. Nobody (besides Joe, maybe) was more surprised than me.

3 Taking the Market by Storm

Creating the Next DQ Blizzard

I haven't been to yoga in nearly three weeks. It seems like the longer I don't go, the harder it is for me to get there. Conversely, the more I go, the more effortless it is. And I'm not talking about the yoga itself, but the actual impetus it requires to give up the comfy couch I've gotten accustomed to and get moving. I'm sure that someone who has never tried to brand something creatively might face a similar issue: How do you turn off the inertia and get moving to find your best brand solution? The first thing you have to do is simply get started.

Think Big, but Start Small

Focusing in before your forge ahead

A few years into our business, we had an assignment with a major food manufacturer that was a definite milestone in my career. It wasn't the project output that was so remarkable, but rather the briefing for it. Up until that point, project kick-off meetings were at least two hours long, involved stacks upon stacks of background information, and outlined specific branding or new product areas for us to explore. Instead of the big conference room kind of meeting, I remember being in this small office with an entire briefing document handed to me on one single sheet. The client said, "People are busier than ever and do not have time to eat hearty and satisfying breakfasts. Create new products that are either 'grab and go' or 'heat and eat' that solve this need." All this with one parameter: "No bagels." Less than thirty minutes later we were on our way back to New York.

My head was overflowing with the opportunities: I could create anything—new forms of cereal, new breads, new pastries, yogurt—anything. I wanted to make sure I had explored each and every flavor, form, and kind of breakfast offering because I knew the answer could be hiding anywhere. With such a big task at hand, I did what anyone else would do: I got stuck. Days went by and this paralysis-by-possibilities did not subside. Suddenly, I real-

ized that I had to narrow my probing or I'd never move forward. I went back to the three main points on that one-page document: "people are too busy for breakfast," "they want something more hearty and satisfying," and "it can be grab-and-go or heat-and-eat." Once I looked at the assignment instead of the possibilities, I was up and running.

I took the notion that "People are too busy for breakfast" and began thinking of brand names and promises that included the word *fast* or *busy* or *quick*. If it worked for Quick Quaker Oats, perhaps a new product would be found here. In the "hearty and satisfying" camp, we could explore adding nuts, cheeses, or other proteins into breads, pastries, and muffins in different ways. For the last section of "grab-and-go or heat-and-eat," I started hypothesizing about different forms that lend themselves to eating while in motion or transit, and how those products would differ if they were hot or cold. (Think of the difference between a cereal bar and a breakfast Hot Pocket.) From narrowing my scope I actually became more productive.

I'm not saying that you shouldn't look far and wide to explore new physical, functional, and emotional territories for your brand to live in. But more important, you have to stop worrying about the infinite possible answers and focus more on what it is you want to end up with.

That's where those two key questions from the briefing

come in. The first being: "What is your Best Wish List for the project?" For this client, it was to have this new breakfast product solve the needs of the busy breakfast eater (or the one too busy to even eat breakfast, for that matter). Your goal might be to create a brand for an existing prototype, to line extend a certain brand, to invent an entire line of products, or to simply capture a great product promise or a tagline that lasts forever.

The second question of "Where can we not go?" proved equally important. One of the great time-wasters of all in new product creation is the notion that the sky really is the limit. Without a clear understanding of the parameters of the project, you risk spending valuable time and energy creating around areas that you know will never get off the ground, for business reasons, cost reasons— any reason. For an idea to be a really good one, it has to be usable, which is why we always work very closely with the folks at Research and Development (R&D) to make sure that the ideas we are coming up with can actually be done. Sometimes, they will consent to one or two ideas that challenge their current capabilities, but, not surprisingly, those are usually the concepts that get the ax early on. Let's face it: Who wants to spend millions of dollars to create a product that requires a new manufacturing process when there are nineteen other products on the table that don't? Knowing where you do—and don't—want to go will not give you the solution to your branding chal-

lenge. However, setting realistic goals and limiting yourself to a reasonably sized playing field will help you know where to look.

This kind of thinking applies not only to very broad new product assignments, it also very much applies to specific ones. When Centrum asked us to reposition the base Centrum brand, we still had to know that we were talking to lapsed vitamin users only and that our messages would talk directly to them. We also had to understand what we realistically could and could not say (e.g., "Take Centrum. Live Forever" probably wouldn't fly).

It's okay to have multiple goals. Sometimes you want to see the difference between a line of products or a single product, or you want to explore how your brand changes when you're talking to different audiences—to me, those exploratories and desires are a part of any good Best Wish List. However, it doesn't hurt to keep your wishes to a reasonable, workable three. (At least three at a time.)

Make a Wish . . . or Three
Identifying the most important goals of a project

Imagine that you had a magic lamp and a genie came out of it and granted you three wishes for your brand or new product. This is not "I want it to be a billion-dollar business" or "I wish for all of my competition to disappear." This is, "If you could accomplish any three things by the end of your project, what would they be?" By asking this, you can understand the expectations for the end of a project right at the beginning of it. Knowing where you want to end up sets the stage for success—whether we're working with clients or you're working on your own.

These were just the kinds of things I wanted to know at a briefing with Dairy Queen when our firm was hired to help it create some new products for its flagship Blizzard brand. According to the Web site, a Blizzard-like product was introduced in DQ franchises in the early 1950s. It started as a shake with less milk, then no milk at all (just fruit and vanilla soft-serve ice cream) but as much as customers liked it, it was a lot of extra work and the super-thick consistency burned out more mixers than franchisees were willing to put up with. Thirty-five years later, regional ice cream shops were creating similar products with milk, ice cream, and candy and the Blizzard had its second go-around (under the name "Concrete Blizzard") but without much more success.

The key to a successful Blizzard came soon after with the introduction of high-powered mixers and the brilliant marketing insight that adding branded candy products would add instant equity at no extra charge. Twenty years, several major brand partnerships, and billions of Blizzards later, the Dairy Queen team was looking for the next big storm to hit the shelves. It had already found much success in its equity-building co-branded endeavors, creating unique and previously unheard-of partnerships with the likes of Oreos, M&Ms, Reese's Peanut Butter Cups, and Snickers. It had introduced many dessert-inspired products, such as the ever-popular Chocolate Chip Cookie Dough Blizzard, the Brownie Batter Blizzard, a line of Cheesequake Blizzards, and even the lesser-known Pumpkin Pie, Egg Nog, and Peanut Butter and Jelly Blizzards. When you think about twenty years of Blizzard-making based on product ingredients and flavors alone, Dairy Queen had run the gamut—and done so quite well. Our job, then, was to help Dairy Queen make the most of its flavor expertise and work with it to create new products that would not only appeal to current Blizzard consumers, but attract new ones as well.

So here were their three wishes:

1. Come up with something more adult/upscale than we already have.
2. Create a Blizzard that could have more perceived value.
3. New textures and consistencies would certainly be a welcome concept.

As you can see, these are not earth-shattering revelations here. But this helped inordinantly to organize my thinking and my approach to finding potential solutions.

If you're reading this book with a specific brand challenge in mind, this might be a good time to write down your own Three Wishes. These are nothing more than where you'd like to end up at the end of, in our case, ten days. If you don't have a specific product in mind, use something on your desk or within your eyesight for right now. It could be a stapler, your favorite pair of jeans, a paper clip, your chair, your cat, the HVAC system in your home. (Don't think too long about this. You can always choose another one later.) Once you've chosen your product, give it Three Wishes. How about a new brand name? Maybe you want to create new line extensions of the brand or product you selected? Are you looking for the new form, design, package, or shape for your object? Write it down and write your wish list for your product.

Here's an example using my stapler:

1. I want to make it hipper than the standard Swingline black-armed version.
2. I want to be able to charge more for a nicer design.
3. It should be easier to load staples and easier to use than the current fare.

Approaching brands creatively is about starting many ideas and filtering through them to find the good ones to develop. You never know where a great idea is going to come from and it's good to get as many half-ideas on the table as you can. Maybe some phrases work or sound better than others. Maybe you hit upon a name or a set of words that evoke just the kind of brand message you're hunting for. The key is to start with a clear understanding of what you are looking for and work within the tight restraints of your promise or idea. This discipline pays off. You will not be overwhelmed by all the possibilities, and you'll have a much better chance at arriving at a great brand solution.

The Hypothesis Zone
Giving your wishes some "what ifs"

I always say that preparing for the workshops is one of the most—if not the most—creative things I do. That's because this is the step where the beginnings of successful ideas happen. The key at this step is to not think about whether you have a solution in mind, the key is to ask the questions. The Hypothesis Zone gives you a chance to look around and see all the different possibilities that exist for any challenge without having to worry exactly how it will play out. (That's what the workshops are for.)

The hypotheses sprout directly from your wish list. You've identified where you want to go, now you're charting the map of ways that *might* get you there. I'm not judging my ideas, I'm not looking for the answer—I'm just trolling for the clues. It's so liberating to come up with ideas with the pressure off. There could be a name you like and you don't know what to do with it, it could be an area you'd like to explore, or simply a question that you'd like to have answered. Actually, I write a lot of my hypotheses as questions because they are still guesses to me. At this phase, you're almost still asking yourself "Is this an idea?"

Let's go back to the Dairy Queen list:

How do I create something more upscale or adult?
   High-end flavors?
   Pastry inspired?
   Create gourmet Blizzard?
   What are other upscale brands?

How do I create a Blizzard with more perceived value?
   Add more ingredients?
   Make bigger (or smaller)?
   Make more of a meal than a treat?
   Partner with more luxury treats?

What are some new textures and consistencies?
   What happens if it is thicker or thinner?
   What are other popular beverage textures?
   What are other successful consistencies in the marketplace?

I supplement my list with at least one full day of hypothesis formulating. I walk through stores to see what's going on in other categories, I flip through magazines, focusing mostly on the ads inside to see if another product has a brand, a promise, a form or any thinking that could be applied to the challenge, I look around my office and my home to see if they spark any new possibilities or inspirations. And even if I'm not sure how these elements are going to work, I jot them down. It's always better to have too much inspiration than not enough.

Try thinking of some hypotheses to your project. I'll do the same with my stapler:

Hipper than the standard Swingline black-armed version.

> *Borrow from success of iMac or iPod?*
> *Explore colors—maybe translucent?*
> *Colored staples?*
> *Create cool dual product with mini Polaroids? Digital camera?*

Charge more for a nicer design.

> *Make designer or designer-inspired?*
> *Make shape more elegant or funky.*
> *What materials besides metal or plastic?*
> *Make match desk or office décor.*

Easier to load staples and easier to use.

Create the "one-touch" stapler.

Borrow some functionality of electric stapler?

Motion sensor?

Create signal before you run out of staples.

Replace whole "staple cartridge" at once.

Usually, I end up with anywhere between forty and seventy bits of potential inspiration—which I've begged, borrowed, created, and stolen from my experience as marketer, consumer, and creative person. Lots of times, these hypotheses are slight variations on a theme, sometimes I have a great name or set of words that I want to create a product from. Other times, they consist of different ways to approach consumer benefit language and preempt new promises. Don't hold back on writing the amount of ways to solve your idea. Think now, judge later. Your list will naturally cull down. You'll see repeat thoughts and ideas, and ones that don't seem as interesting or promising as others. For me, the list gets shortened the most when I get to the next step of turning hypotheses into workshop exercises. Either I realize that I've just fallen in love with a set of words rather than a real idea, or I have trouble starting a thought based on my own thought-starter. A good rule of thumb is, if you can't imagine at least one answer, then you might skip that hypothesis.

So let's take a look at how to take strategic speculation and turn it into branding and new product inspiration.

The Workshop Workout
Turning hypotheses into idea-generating exercises

If I just stopped there I'd have a pretty good jumping-off point for creating concepts and potential strategic areas to explore. But why walk away from creative momentum? I've identified where I want to go, I've come up with a few ways of getting there, and now I'm in the perfect state of mind to begin solution hunting.

I take what I consider the most exciting and meaning-ful hypotheses and turn them into a format of approxi-mately thirty creative exercises that I will use in my Workshop Workout. That means taking each one of those notes from the list above and posing it so that it elicits the most creative solutions per area. If the exercise is not in-spiring, I may miss out on the perfect solution. Also, if the hypothesis is too broad, the responses will be mediocre and wishy-washy. This step is important whether you have the luxury of running creative groups or not. In the same way that I pose the questions to others, you can use these creative techniques to elicit new ideas from your own brain.

Here's how it works: Take my last hypothesis of "other textures and consistencies." What you don't want to do is simply pose the question as: "What would be other textures and consistencies that the Blizzard could be?" Instead, I might take one of those consistencies and try to find the best way to communicate it in the marketplace. In its simplest form, it's as easy as posing the question: "This new Blizzard is the creamiest treat on earth. Create an appealing name and rally cry that gives it utter taste and imagery appeal." My name would be "Creamy Dreamy" and my rally cry would be "Heaven has arrived." What about yours?

If every workshop exercise was that straightforward, it wouldn't be long before the creative energy would start to wane. That's why each exercise should be a little different from the one before, with different thought-starters, mind-openers, and elements of creative inspiration that keep the interest of the participants—as well as their output—at a maximum. I do not have a single boilerplate format that I plug different words into here and there. That would result in cookie-cutter ideas born from cookie-cutter thinking. That's not to say I don't have favorites. Following are some of those exercises that work well no matter what the challenge.

Prop It Up

A simple visual stimulus helps focus and inspire creative thinking

A friend of mine has a wry, insightful blog called "Anthropologist for Corporate America: Multitasking My Way to

Inner Peace." From her subtitle, you might gather the tongue-in-cheek-yet-sadly-true idiosyncrasies of today's corporate environment that she writes about. She works for one of the major computer network companies, and we were talking about how every brainstorming meeting she endures starts with a clear set of goals (think our Best Wish List), but it is only a matter of time before people lose sight of them. Each person has his or her own real agenda. These agendas come complete with favorite ideas, personal priorities, egos, and lots of baggage to boot. Before you know it, there are so many tangents going on, it's three hours later and precious little has been accomplished.

An essential part of successful single-minded brainstorming is the ability to concentrate on one area at a time. Every meeting needs an anchor, a focal point, and something that will help put tangents to the side, where they (by definition) belong. I use related props that represent the idea or hand out pictures that literally get everyone on the same page. For example, if I wanted to have a brand message whose main benefit was flexibility, I might hold up a Gumby doll, show a picture of a Cirque du Soleil performer, or even pass out rubber bands to each participant.

If I'm looking for a multitasking product or name, we might show a Swiss Army knife or a picture of an octopus.

The most important thing is that the item has to work

with the proposition, or else you'll have everyone focusing in on the wrong idea.

If you were going to choose an object or visual to help the thinking center around creating a high-end Blizzard for Dairy Queen, what would you choose? Better yet, why not choose an appropriate prop or visual for one or more of the hypotheses on your list? We got some of those paper hats that chefs wear for the workshop participants, and used those as our thinking caps. (In the voice of a chef, each person had to tell us his or her new gourmet Blizzard and give it a great name. What would your chef creation be?)

What about the stapler? I might show an iMac or iPod

advertisement and have participants create a similar visual communication for our line of funky staplers. I might show a bottle of Skyy vodka to illustrate the importance of color to a brand. And if I make the vodka the prize as well, it's amazing how quickly people will focus in on it. Even if you are doing this by yourself, it is helpful to have a point of inspiration (not to be confused with Inspiration Point where Richie Cunningham from *Happy Days* took his dates).

Another way to use props and pictures is the "I Spy" approach. Look around wherever you are right now and ask yourself if there is something around you that might bring you one step closer to the answer you are looking for.

Finish This _____.
Putting your words in someone else's mouth

One of my biggest pet peeves is when people refer to our workshops as focus groups and not creative workshops. True, both involve a conference table with consumers around it and some free food, but that's where the similarities end. Focus groups ask for opinions, which is rarely—if ever—what we want to get involved with. Asking opinions at the conceptual stage of the game is inviting in the marketing equivalent of Pandora's pandemic. How do I know? Ask ten people about anything—having wisdom teeth removed, how they feel about flying, what they thought about the latest Tom Hanks movie—and everyone will tell you something different. Opinions are not great creative fodder, even though we want to bring in ideas that are based on people's personal experiences and knowledge. So how do we accomplish that?

That's where our imaginary friend, Janie, comes in. I often use an exercise where I explain that Janie called me on the phone with the beginning of an idea, but that the connection was broken (damn cell phones!) before I heard the rest of the idea. I then ask the group to figure out the rest of whatever Janie happened to be talking about on that particular day. Sometimes, the missing element is a name; e.g., Janie said "I love this new soft drink because it is so fresh tasting. No wonder they call it _____." Other times, it is an emotion; e.g., Janie said, "I love this new credit card because it makes me feel _____."

Or in this case, Janie is a Blizzard lover who everyone thinks is crazy because she replaces one meal a day with the new Blizzard product. What could possibly be in the Blizzard that allows her to do that? If everyone independently fills in the blank in a similar way, we know that those are the answers that fit more intuitively with the product. The other scenario is just as good: A wide range of answers means more creative opportunities for us.

Using this technique is a great trick and a no lose proposition. First of all, we avoid the ignorant, knee-jerk (opinion-laden) responses such as "Well, I would never eat a Blizzard as a meal" that come had we put the word "you" in Janie's place. Second, we steer clear of being forced to sit through every anecdote and the not-so-brief history of the new product itself. And this mode is contagious. The more one person does it, the more everyone wants to share his or her story. Before you know it, an hour has passed and you're still listening to how every summer, mom made someone finish his or her veggies before taking the family station wagon to Dairy Queen.

For the Blizzard, Janie helped get many new ingredient combinations and great names for products that suggested more satisfaction and a less sweet treat. Logic told us that the secret was definitely in the mix-ins—nuts, fruits, yogurts, whole grains, and granola suggest a healthier option than their candy-filled cousins. All we needed was to choose from a lot of great naming and imagery that would carry the day. Because so many Dairy Queen franchises are drive-thrus and SUVs were so popular at the time, it's no wonder we landed here:

Blaze your day.

Fuel your day deliciously.

The SUV of Blizzard treats.

One of my favorite parts of this concept was the fact that we had taken the tree-hugging, Jamba-Juice enthusiast's smoothie and gave it some real Blizzard flair. This was a non-frou-frou, gender-neutral product that had functional appeal and Blizzard fun wrapped into one. However, introducing more ingredients for franchisees to stock and low consumer purchase-intent is what made it the second concept of the twenty to get the official "no-go" (which is why I can show it here). In this case, it was the consumers *and* operators that said, "Blaze your day elsewhere."

But don't give up on Janie just because this idea didn't work. Her sentence-starters have helped us get people out of their heads and into ours more than once. In fact, Janie called us this morning from her cell phone and told us that she loves the feature on her new stapler that tells her when she's about to run out of staples. Her cell phone signal ran out, so we had to just guess what that feature was. Can you think of at least one? Good, then Janie's done her job.

Branding at 65 mph
If you can say it on a billboard, you're on to something

My friend hates—really hates—the old Michelin tire ads, the ones with the cute babies rolling around the tires. "It's absurd," he tells me. "Babies don't drive cars! What's worse, I actually understand why it works. The message is clear: If you don't buy our tires, your kid may die in a car crash. I resent that ploy."

What's he talking about? Most of the time, I have some of the same hesitations with this visual image as my friend does. However, marketing is rarely, if ever, based solely on logic. It relies on the emotion—the visceral reaction—that instant connection with an audience that only the illogical can create. That's why thinking visually can be so important. It's not that a picture says a thousand words. It's that your picture can trigger an emotion inside the brain of a consumer that is so powerful no amount of words would be able to express it. Michelin created a simple visual icon of its brand message—safety. It did it without crash-test dummies or statistics or technical specifications; just a few diaper-clad toddlers and everyone got it, like it or not. As for my friend, the agency that created the ad would say that it was effective. Even though he hated the ad, he remembered the brand and its promise many years after the campaign ended.

Asking people to create this kind of quick, distinct visual imagery around a certain hypothesis can be very productive. Even though I present my work as if it were two-page introductory ads, in truth I'm always striving for the billboard. With the billboard, the disciplines of the print ad become magnified. You may be forced to convey your message using just one word or one visual cue to get your brand message across.

Let's take a break from Blizzards and take a hypothesis from the stapler. Which message would you select to try to convey on a billboard? (Don't have the billboard say just anything. You still need to give people a point of focus.) In truth, a lot of them could work, but I choose to put on the billboard the fact that this stapler could be a one-touch solution. Think about that: If you had to create a picture with only a visual that said you could staple papers with just one touch, what would it be?

Maybe you would put the stapler balancing on one person's finger, or maybe you would show other "one-

So here's your billboard. Which hypothesis from your list would you choose
to make the perfect billboard exercise? And how would you fill it in?

touch" things like an elevator button or doorbell and feature the stapler in the line-up. Or maybe just a visual of
someone who is snapping his or her fingers in that "it's a
snap" kind of way. Each idea gets us thinking not only of
potential product attributes (activating a stapler with a
button being one of them), but also of names (a stapler
called "Snap," perhaps) and visually enduring themes
(such as the balancing act).

There's a second exercise here if you're looking for
words instead, or in addition to the visual. Imagine that
you're driving down the highway and you see the same

billboard from the other direction. The message is the same, but this time there was no visual, just one, two, or three words that were equally as powerful. What were they?

For the Michelin tires, maybe the words would have been "Protect what matters." For my stapler, maybe they would have been "Just add finger" or "One touch wonderful." What about for your product?

Blizzard by the Numbers

Finding the magic number could be just the thing

Maybe it's because I'm the daughter of an engineer, or maybe it's because I actually liked my algebra teacher in high school, but there's something about using numbers as a source for ideas that I've always found particularly fascinating.

In branding and new product creation, the ability to own a particular number is invaluable. Think about the difference between a "blended vegetable drink" and "V8." From the name, you know that there are eight kinds of vegetables in every container. Heinz 57 explains on its Web site that in 1896 H. J. Heinz arbitrarily turned "more than 60 products into '57 Varieties.'" The magic number became world renowned and now is virtually synonymous with the H. J. Heinz Company. You can also use numbers as a source for new product and brand ideas. Start with the number first and see where it takes you.

Numbers can evoke any number of things, from ingredients, such as 5 Alive juice drinks; time it takes to use, such as the Aussie 5-Minute Miracle or One-a-Day vitamins; and numbers can also be totally made up. The Oil of Olay brand created their "7 Signs of Aging" only to have their lotions contain the ingredients that treat them all. Car companies do it all the time with their 3000, 6000, and 9000 model cars. Software developers use numbers to show newer versions and editions. Razor brands use the number of blades they have to suggest efficacy, which is why we have the Mach3 from Gillette only to be outdone by the Quattro from Schick, which has been (temporarily?) trumped with the five-bladed Fusion from Gillette.

There's a risk here: When the number means something specific, such as a sale number, an interest rate, or something that can be easily one-upped by a competitor, it's better to look elsewhere. Also, when thinking about numbers, be wary of using numbers like 2000, especially in our postmillennium world. The Dilbert cartoon featured a product called the Gruntmaster 6000. You don't need me to tell you that if your product sounds like a Dilbert cartoon, run. Today's auto manufacturers have changed their names from thousands to more understated numbers like Audi's A7, A5, and A3.

For Blizzard, I was guessing that the number could play a role in adding perceived value. If the name of the new Blizzard product had the number "1" in it, what would it be about? One big ingredient? One slurp? One with everything? How about the numbers 2, 3, or 5?

During the workshop, we got everyone into teams of twos and asked them to create a name and a product based on the number of people in their team. It's amazing what a difference one number can make. The teams of two readily came up with Double Trouble, Blizzard Twins, and Delicious Duos, but our favorite name was Double Dare. Once one of the DQ employees said it, we imagined that the dare aspect was really half of the idea.

I double dare you not to like this idea.

The "double" idea didn't work as well for consumers as it did for us. True to the past Blizzard success, there is typically one flavor or combination of flavors that attracts consumers and putting twice as much in didn't raise the bar any farther. It's no wonder that our "Triple Happiness" Blizzards also did not test well.

In most cases, however, numbers can help formulate your product's promise and turn what could be a parity product into something that has a clear point-of-difference.

So pick a number. Any number. And include that in your Workshop Workout. If you're feeling indecisive, use the number 3.

Eyes Wide Shut
Visualizing the sights, smells, and sounds of a fresh idea

Here's a quick test: While you're reading this, imagine that you're at a restaurant and you are served an indulgent dessert and you really love it. What is it? Write it down.

Now try the same exercise again, but this time close your eyes and transport yourself anywhere in the world. Imagine the smells, the sounds, and the kind of tastes that place evokes. Keep your eyes shut for at least fifteen seconds for the whole picture to come together in your mind. Let your dessert truly come from that place.

Now write down your answer. How is it different?

Chances are that by closing your eyes and mentally putting yourself in another place, you gave your mind a chance to escape your physical surroundings. You were no longer relying on your brainpower, rather tapping into your memories and imagination, which is far more powerful. Furthermore, the success of the brand itself is often tied to the place that inspired it, and can spark similarly powerful images in the minds of consumers.

Take a look and see how your location-inspired answer was similar or different to ours.

As you can see, we wanted to bring the tropical look

The coolest tastes from the hottest places.

and appeal to every aspect of our communication, without losing the fun and flavors that define the Blizzard brand. Plus, because Dairy Queen and Orange Julius are both owned by the same parent company, we were hoping that some corporate symbiosis would occur. However, this idea was not new or unique enough to get it off the ground.

Obviously, an island is by far not the only—or most—creative or interesting place on earth. Maybe we could have gone on an imaginary road trip to a place in the continental United States that might bring to mind regionalized combinations and imagery. We could have transported ourselves to a fancy restaurant or famous amusement park that might have given more energy, more excitement to this idea.

Where would you go to find one of the answers on your list? Is it a place? A decade? A state of mind? It's a funny example to try with the stapler, but I'll give it a shot. Since I know that one of my goals is to create a new and elegant design, I'm going to imagine it as if it were a sculpture in a modern art gallery. Try it, too. Really close your eyes and open your mind to what that would look like. (Mine was black and glossy, and stood up vertically. It closed like a clamshell, so that you couldn't tell it was a stapler until you opened it up. Camouflage desk art . . . I might be on to something.)

Borrow Their Equity
Find success where other brands already have

Based on the history of the Blizzard and its success borrowing from the equity of others, I should have guessed that our brand-borrowing workshop technique would produce the first of our new product ideas to hit their stores. This technique involves either choosing a specific brand or letting participants make a list of their favorite brands in other categories and choose at least one as the fictitious brand sponsor. You can see how a Tiffany's Blizzard (white chocolate, simple, elegant flavors) might feature different textures and ingredients from a Whole Foods Blizzard (organic, earth-friendly), a Nike Blizzard (made with juice for athletes), or a Home Depot Blizzard (let customers add their own ingredients). But instead of just creating any new Blizzard, I was on a mission to create a high-end, indulgent Blizzard and with that I needed some heavy-duty imagery help. Which is why Victoria's Secret became my fake brand-sponsor of choice.

Imagine that you were walking through Victoria's Secret when you saw a display featuring these amazingly indulgent line of Blizzards, featured only in their stores. There was something romantic, something special, something indulgent about these cool, creamy offerings that were unlike any other. What was it? Think of the imagery first, and then create the name. (Remember, this is not about sex, lingerie, or anything "secret.")

By framing the name in the context of a recognized brand, I'm helping participants visualize a product that might actually exist. I'm also helping them break out of the natural constraints that might come from their current expectations and ingredient-centric thinking of what constitutes a Blizzard today.

The Dairy Queen team was very inventive. The employees, who created many of the winning concepts, also came up with many incredible Victoria's Secret-inspired answers, from death by chocolate, divalike Blizzards to subtle, sensuous "Whispers" that were slightly thinner, lighter, and more delicate than the usual fare. The one we developed was the name and concept of the "Blissard," which is such a perfect fit with the Victoria's Secret brand (see next page).

What frequently happens with our work is that the final iteration is not the same as the original concept. That's because clients will test and refine our output until our creative ideals work for their marketplace reality. In the case of the Blissard, consumers didn't like the name, but they went ga-ga (industry term) over the upscale chocolate flavors listed on the concept. (Who wouldn't? Good thing these are launching soon at a Dairy Queen near you.) What that told the marketing mavens at Dairy

Fall in love.

BLIZZARD

Blissard

100% pure bliss.

Fall in love with the new Bliss at DQ.

Queen was that the imagery and appeal of boutiquelike chocolates was hot, but the fake-sounding French names were not. That's okay for us, because success can come from any element of a concept and today's savvy consumers are getting better and better at expressing which elements work for them.

Could we have come across this upscale concept without Victoria's Secret? It's possible. I could have evoked the indulgent, exclusive personality of New York City's Serendipity treat shop, or maybe another participant would have pieced together three upscale flavors during the numbers exercise.

Either way, the more of these kinds of exercises you do, the more ways you will find to bring your hypotheses to the next level. Each project we have inspires new exercises, new props, and new ways to get to the answers we seek. Once I wanted to have our product inspire trust so I had a participant do a quick "trust" fall into the arms of someone else. Joe recently created an exercise that was all about this unexpected bonus, where a person leaves the room for three seconds, and we yell "Surprise" when they come back in. With a little more experience, you'll see why we say that writing the format for the workshops and inventing the exercises is just as creative—if not more so—than anything else we do.

Now what?
You've got the ideas, now bring them to life

After the workshops are finished, the first thing we do is take a step back and look at which ideas inspire us the most and put our thinking back into more generalized, conceptual terms. That means that instead of just loving my black shiny stapler objet d'art, I would itemize that concept as "camouflage desk art"—instead of the actual idea—that I'd keep in my notes. I do that in order to make sure that the concept itself goes beyond the single idea that started it. The last thing I want to do is fall in love with a cute tagline, visual, or product idea that has no legs and, frankly, no real backbone either.

Once we have reviewed our list of conceptual directions with our client, we are off and running to take all these pieces, parts, and bits of ideas and begin to put them together with the right verbal and visual messages. In other words, we're at the point where we're taking the ideas and bringing them to life, which is exactly what the next chapter is all about.

What's Your Line?

*Writing the Perfect Headline, Tagline—
or Both*

I am perpetually amazed by the poor concept-writing skills of marketing types. I have seen hundreds of concepts that have a headline that starts with "Introducing," "If you ever thought," or "Try the new," and have some kind of tagline at the end, like "The Cleaner that Is Easier to Use," "Enjoying Moments Together," or sadly, "So Go Ahead and Buy One Today." In between are marketing insights linked together in disjointed sentences that read like a book report written by a foreign exchange student. By the time a consumer reads through it, they don't know whether to be bored or confused.

How did this happen? Since when did smart, savvy marketers forget how to talk to their audience?

Most of the problem lies in the fact that most concepts are written to satisfy market research imperatives. This means that every concept must include consumer insight, reason to believe, key product attribute, how and when product fits into life, what need it solves—essentially, a lot of information written on a level that most consumers don't relate to. It's a very logical approach to concept writing, and selling a product or brand is not always a logical endeavor. When consumers buy products and services, they're reacting to a particular promise, not to the brilliant train of logic that lurks behind the message. This market research trap contributes to the dry, uncomfortable, non-flowing writing styles of most concepts today. While I could give a few pointers on that (e.g., read your copy out loud and see if it sounds like normal consumer English), the harder thing to do is to communicate your selling message in a short, concise headline, tagline, or rally cry that will capture your true brand message, so let's focus on that first.

There's a joke that "sarchasm" is the gap between a joke you tell and someone else not getting it. I would add that there exists a "brandchasm" between what you want to say about your product and how well consumers hear it. People do not have attention spans that last forever.

You have to make your message matter—and do it quickly. These are the reasons for headlines and taglines.

"Hey wait a minute," you must be wondering. "What's the difference between a headline and a tagline? And isn't that advertising and not branding?"

Good questions. My partner would say that the more enduring, more favorite set of words should be the headline, since usually it is the biggest type on the page. I disagree. I believe that the headline should relate directly to the visual. In the case of an all-text ad, the headline should work as the attention getter, just as it would on a newspaper or cover of a magazine. The tagline, for me, is the set of words that go with the logo or the product at the bottom of the page, that should always be able to wrap up the main idea of the concept and, in the best-case scenario, should be so powerful that you could take everything else off the page and still know what the concept is about.

There are times when these rules do not apply. Sometimes the headline and tagline are truly interchangeable, and, in the hierarchy of things, it's more important *how* you convey your selling message than *where* you convey it. Lots of times, you don't know until the visual is in place to see which one should go where, and we often move them around.

This also relates to how our branding taglines and

concepts differ from advertising concepts. Our main goal is to have each concept relay one message in true consumer language. Once tested, an ad agency usually takes that message and builds an ad campaign from it. Our goal is to make our message heard quickly. Their goal is to make the message heard creatively. That's not to say that our headlines and taglines cannot and have not been used in ad and brand campaigns. I would argue—and often do—that there's wisdom in having an advertising slogan that's more communicative than clever.

There are many ways to approach successful, persuasive brand messages that can give your product, service, or company the ability to get through to your consumers quickly and effectively. Many companies come to us with just this kind of assignment. One such client was BriteSmile whitening. It had a name, a new product, and a marketplace that couldn't get their teeth white enough. What it needed was a brand message that would break through the ever-growing whitening noise.

BriteSmile was introducing a revolutionary White Light whitening technology developed by the same scientist who pioneered the Lasik eye-surgery technology. The treatment—start to finish—took less than one hour and, at the time, cost about $600.

Sounds great, right? But here's the problem: The shelves of the drug store and mass market chains are filled with whitening products up the wazoo—strips, bleaching kits, mouth rinses, chewing gums, not to mention that nearly every brand of toothpaste offers a whitening option. So not only are these products more accessible, they're also much more affordable (the most expensive one being $40 at most). And all of these products, including BriteSmile, essentially make the same promise: We will make your teeth whiter than they are now. BriteSmile needed the right message that was going to make its whitening product shine above the rest.

Make It Newsworthy

Attention-grabbing headlines from those who make headlines

True story: I was professionally photographed to appear in an issue of *Men's Health* magazine. I was told they were doing an article called "Find the Perfect Wife: Pages of Women Who Are Amazing—and Amazingly—Still Single." Luckily, my photo was not chosen, because when the magazine hit the stands the title of the article had changed to: "Find the Perfect Sex Partner." Once you looked inside, the revised subtitle explained that the perfect sex partner is usually a long-time mate, which could be a wife. Obviously, the writers at *Men's Health* know the importance of grabbing your attention, and it stands to reason that your product could benefit from this kind of thinking.

Now, of course I'm not saying that you should falsely advertise your service, or that you should use sex to sell your product (although that works, too). Rather, titles of magazine and newspaper articles are designed to grab your attention, they let you know what the article is about, and most important, they usually do it using fewer than five words.

When making a workshop exercise that involves headline news, it helps to first identify what is truly new or different about your product. Let's look at BriteSmile. Whitening? With so many other products on the shelves, whitening alone was not news. The fact that it only took one hour while the others took weeks . . . now that was news we could use.

Different brands of news offer different voices. We use the voice of the *Daily News* when we want to be clever and sensational (White Away!), the *New York Times* when we want to be straightforward and sophisticated (The Fastest White in the World), and popular fashion and beauty magazines when looking for some real consumer appeal (The White You've Been Waiting For). Since BriteSmile was a cosmetic treatment, we placed our article about this new one-hour whitening product in the pages of *Self* magazine.

Imagine for one second that *Self* magazine had an article about this amazing one-hour whitening experience. The title of the article was so eye-catching, so newsworthy, that you couldn't help but read on. What do you imagine the title was?

There are a few ways to go here. You could go for the short title and long subtitle, such as "White Now: The 60 Minutes that Will Make You Smile" or have the title tell the whole story, such as "White Without the Wait." Either one works just fine; and, in fact, we got a lot of both from the workshops. There was the "One-Hour Whitening Miracle," "Just One Hour to White," "Make One Hour Last for Years," "One Hour to a More Beautiful You." Here were the same people who wrote bad concepts suddenly writing great headlines!

Then someone blurted out "Instant Gratification," which opened up a whole new area of thinking. Would "instant" be an overpromise or just the right amount of exaggeration? How important was the one-hour treatment versus the consumer benefit of seeing results quickly? The only way to find out was to try them both.

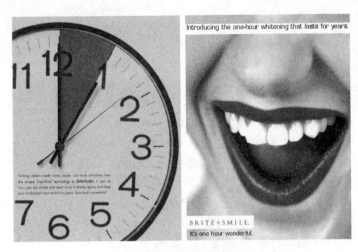

It's all about the hour.

Hour + Results = A better concept.

For argument's sake, let's look for a second at the placement of the headline and taglines here before we go on. If we move the "one hour wonderful" tagline to the forefront of the first concept, what happens? It's okay, but it gives the wrap-up without telling the story first. "The one-hour whitening that lasts for years" is a pretty good claim and, if this is all we want to say about their one-hour difference, then it should be relegated to the tagline. By placing the tagline where it currently is, it allows the client to say any number of things in the future about what makes our one hour so wonderful.

In the second concept, I think the headline and tagline are more interchangeable, since "instant gratification" is a powerful and succinct message that needs no more explaining when used with the name BriteSmile. We relegated it to headline status because it spoke to the picture more; and, further, because "one hour to a beautiful smile" stands up to the ultimate test of telling exactly what the concept is about even if the rest of the concept weren't there.

When hunting for the news of your product, you can pick an attribute (such as one hour), but you can also let the publication dictate the news. If the *Wall Street Journal* were writing an article, they might write about this new standard of whitening within the industry. *Popular Science* might talk about the second brainchild of the Lasik genius. So sometimes finding the "right" publication can be as interesting an exercise in branding as writing the head-line itself.

Look Who's Talking

First person, second person, and third person headlines.
When to use each and why.

How successful would the "I could have had a V8" tagline have been if it were used in the second- or third-person voices? Try it. It doesn't work that well at all. What if that ever-famous Miss Clairol line was changed from "Does she . . . or doesn't she?" to "Do you . . . or don't you?" The power of these brand messages relies on precisely who is saying it. And yet the cosmetic giant L'Oréal has success-fully changed its powerhouse line from "Because I'm worth it" to "Because you're worth it." What's going on here?

Using different narrative perspectives can have an im-pact on the tone of your brand, and gives you a good way to avoid the common pitfalls of personality-free concept statements. Knowing when and how to use them is a mat-ter of taste, common sense, and bit of trial and error.

It seems logical to look at the first person, well . . . first.

In general, I avoid using the first person. I believe that unless the idea is all about a testimonial approach (i.e., a satisfied-sleepers campaign for Sealy called "Restimonials" begs for first person expressions), you shouldn't have people talking—especially if you can help it. On television when you can have a real person saying the line, it may work better but, in a print concept, it typically leaves you with a nondescript person smiling into the "camera" as the puppet for your strategy-du-jour.

There are exceptions to my disdain for the first person and that's when you really want your target audience to relate to a very specific emotion or experience that only another person can feel. When Apple Computer was trying to convert PC users to switch to Macintosh products, it ran a series of commercials that featured testimonials from down-to-earth people who told a light-hearted story about their experience with their PC. It was obvious from their tone and their use of the past tense that their troubles were over. They would say things like "It spent more time crashing than working," or "Sometimes I just wanted to bang my head against the wall," or "It turned me into a full-time IT guy,"—all with smiles on their faces that told the world that their computer troubles were a thing of the past.

The only other nice thing about first-person headlines is that once you have the right emotion, it's a quick and easy change to a meaningful third-person tagline, as you'll see in the following two concepts for BriteSmile.

I got the best smile ever
in just one hour.

Rich Jennings,
Atlanta, Georgia

Multiple independent clinical studies prove that the **BriteSmile** procedure works better than anything else out there. It's only available from the dentist, but was better than anything I had ever tried at home. In just one hour, my smile looked the whitest, brightest, and best it had looked in years. So join me and the over 300,000 others who have seen their best smiles since the revolutionary technology was made available 3 years ago.

BRITE SMILE.
Get your best smile ever. Guaranteed.

I'm always testy about using testimonials,
but once in a while I try it anyhow.

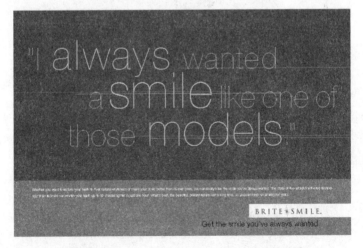

"I always wanted
a smile like one of
those models."

Whether you want to capture your health's final natural whiteness or make your smile better than it's ever been, you can analyze how the smile you've always wanted. The state of the art teeth whitening technology that is only available from your dentist can whiten your teeth up to 8-10 shades lighter in just one hour. What's more, the beautiful, brilliant results last a long time, so you can keep smiling for years.

BRITE SMILE.
Get the smile you've always wanted.

Does connecting with an emotion make it work better?

Now let's take a look at these two concepts and see how they differ. The first one is a perfect example of the kind of guy-smiling-who-could-be-selling-anything iterations. Who is this guy? Why should I believe him? This guy is just saying what is, in my opinion, a phony baloney testimonial. (Really, who talks like that?) The second concept at least comes closer to giving a specific emotional reason *why* people would choose BriteSmile, and suggests that other reasons such as "I wanted to look nice for my daughter's wedding" or "My high school reunion was just around the corner" could follow in subsequent communications.

Here is a good test you can use to see if using first-person voice is actually working in your favor: Try not using it and see what happens. When you turn "I got the best smile ever in just one hour" to "Get the best smile ever in just one hour," it actually sounds like a great product promise—one I would believe from a company more than an individual. Conversely, when you change "I always wanted a smile like one of those models" to "Get a smile like one of those models," it starts to sound patronizing and loses the approachable, human element that it once evoked. However, the tagline "Get the smile you've always wanted" allows for any number of personal reasons you want to include and balances the headline out just right.

There's another way that companies and products use the first person, and that's in the tagline. This is different than having the person in the concept speak because now the product or corporate entity has gained the uncanny ability to express itself. You can see I am not a fan of this mode because it borders on the self-serving and self-congratulatory. Panasonic used to own the tagline "Just slightly ahead of our time," McDonald's tries to bring a consumer voice to its megalith franchise by saying "I'm lovin' it," and GE proudly proclaimed for many years that "We bring good things to life." At least GE included some consumer benefit within its self-congratulation.

Even worse is the rampant "using of the gerund"—when you use a verb with no subject and add "ing" to the end. Toyota is "Moving you forward" (first and second person in one line) and Nokia is "Connecting people." If you find yourself writing this way, just kill yourself, or at least rip up your legal pad. My disdain for this mode comes from the self-congratulatory, self-praising, seriously superior tone this kind of tagline suggests. Admittedly, Toyota did include the consumer ("you") in its grand moving scheme. But what if it (Toyota) focused the entire message on the consumer? Maybe it would read: "Get in. Be Moved." If Nokia stopped worrying about what it was doing and went to more promise-based language, it might inspire people to "Connect more. Connect better." Other companies have wised up to this, as it was nearly impossible to find any company that had one of these taglines and hasn't yet changed it. Cisco systems changed its "Empowering the Internet generation" to the Intel-inspired "Powered by Cisco." Lucent Technologies went from "Creating value through true convergence" to the less-oblique-but-not-much-more "Networks that know."

The real problem with first person taglines is that they direct the focus away from the consumer and back to the manufacturer or product. It's corporate narcissism at its best (or worst) and rarely works. Dick Damrow and Bob Sevier point out that on the *BusinessWeek*/Interbrand Top 100 Global Brands, only five companies use slogans that end in -ing, and an equally low number use the first person in theirs. I just spent a full hour trying to hunt them down and only found the four examples I just mentioned.

So let's move on to person number two.

Most headlines are written in the second person, or the "you" narrative. It's logical because we want our products and their promises to speak to our audience. The "you" narrative literally brings the person into the conversation. "You deserve a break today," "Just do it," "You and us," "Betcha can't eat just one." Instead of having your brand talk to itself, now you're reaching out. It's such a natural way to talk—especially in English when the "you" form is used to talk about people in particular and in general as in "*You* can't take it with *you*."

When you write any headline or tagline in the second-person voice, it's important that the voice is quick, sincere, and—above all—human. Back to those bad positioning statements that say things like "You work hard all day and often want a time out to get back to the things that matter most to you." This is not a headline. However, "Get back to what matters most" could work just fine.

Let's see how you do creating a second-person headline or tagline for BriteSmile, with a little creative inspiration from our friends at L'Oréal. Its "Because you're worth it" gave deserving women a real justification to spend more money on themselves. Similarly, BriteSmile comes with a steep price tag, and we want to see if a little of the L'Oréal charm can rub off on it. What would be that five-word headline, tagline, or rally cry that would tell women—and men—that they deserved the best whitening treatment?

Who doesn't deserve the best? Our L'Oréal approach.

Again, the headlines and taglines here could switch around. Our creative preference was to have the tagline work more like the L'Oreal brand of communication, where the sign-off talks directly to the reader or listener. How would this concept be different if it were used in the third person?

Technically, the third person is a narrative voice and, like the first person, doesn't always make sense in concept writing. If the last concept read "Best herself" or "She deserves the best," it totally ignores that the reader of the concept is even there. There is a way to use the third person successfully, which is in the role of the admirer or voyeur.

Whether we like it or not, we are constantly prey to the judgments of those around us. (It's ironic since most of us are too busy worrying about how others perceive us to notice what others are doing.) We put on lipstick before going to the grocery store, we want to be heard ordering Ketel One vodka and seen with the latest designer label across our pockets.

And that's where the third person comes in. It appeals to our real sense of vanity that comes into play when we go out and spend our hard-earned cash, especially on discretionary items.

The third person is the voice of those around us, wondering "Does she or doesn't she?" "Is she born with it or is it Maybelline?" We know to "never let 'em see [us] sweat" and that it's important that others "never know you even have dandruff!" Impulse body spray had a different take on the third person, and built a very memorable brand message on the line "If somebody you've never met before suddenly gives you flowers . . ." Cheesy? Yes. Effective and memorable? Double yes.

With BriteSmile, being noticed was a double-edged sword—you wanted people to notice that your teeth were white and bright, but you didn't want them to look too white or too bright. One thing they had told us about in the briefing was that after people get a treatment, others around them notice an improvement, but often have trouble pinpointing exactly what has changed. Did they get a haircut? A new outfit? Did they lose weight? We loved using these questions as part of our brand message. We imagined that the concept would show a person with a great smile together with any one of the previous questions being wondered about her.

"Is that a new shirt?"

Everyone will wonder what it is about you that makes you look different. The state-of-the-art technology at **BriteSmile** restores your teeth to their natural, radiant whiteness to give you the smile that will make you look and feel better every day. So next time someone tries to guess what's so different about you, just smile.

BRITE❀SMILE.
The difference is remarkable.

Getting noticed, just not too much.

Incidentally, Crest White Strips ran some TV ads featuring a *Sex and the City* scenario of four women chatting at a chichi meal. While one woman talks, we hear the voices in the other women's minds as they try to discern why she's smiling so much. New boyfriend? New job? New outfit? As it turns out, she was smiling because she was proud of her new, whiter smile.

One thing that we typically do—especially with a first- or third-person headline—is balance it out with a more general, umbrella message in the tagline. It gives the concept a good balance of personal connection (in the headline) and brand authority (with the product or name, where it should be).

The best way to find out if a first-, second-, or third-person narrative works for your brand is to simply try it out. Just like we've done with some of the previous concepts, you can experiment with different voices and see which one makes the most sense, which one is the most persuasive, and which ones sounds the best to you. Never forget your inner consumer when doing this kind of work.

Got White?
Let your visual do the talking

I was traveling around the wine region of upstate New York, and I came upon these "Got wine?" cocktail napkins in one of the wineries. A good friend of mine has worked on the "Got Milk?" brand for a long time (and is a co-author of two milk-mustache books), and so I couldn't resist buying them for him. He said he would add it to his collection of Gots, along with the "Got Jesus?" T-shirt, the "Got Sod?" lawn-care ad, and his "Got feet?" novelty socks, to name a few. (If idea theft is the sincerest form of flattery, my friend has been flattered to the nth degree.)

Everyone has his or her reason for admiring this campaign. It undoubtedly has given us one of the most memorable and successful taglines and enduring visuals of our time. Why it's pertinent here is how the milk-mustache campaign used spokespeople and celebrities to do the talking for them.

Its ads feature celebrities who drink milk, along with specific reasons why they choose to drink milk. Put a white, frothy mustache on a celebrity, and you've got the winning formula. The brilliance of this idea is worth flattering with a little creative imitation.

Often in the workshops, we evoke the milk-mustache campaign when we want to create an enduring visual that includes a person with the product. The person can be a celebrity, like in the milk campaign, or just an everyday person. I remember creating an enduring visual of green lips for a menthol cigarette, a rippled tongue for Ruffles potato chips, and skin tattoo for a brand of lotion. I'm not saying these ideas were anywhere near as effective as the milk mustache, just that I've tried them.

I think we came a little closer with BriteSmile. It actually had real celebrities who used its process, and we wanted to take full advantage of this fact. What would we say? How would we do it? What would be the most enduring, most interesting, most clever visual that would let the celebrity smiles speak for us? Any ideas? Are there a few words you can create that work perfectly with your visual?

The idea that came out of the workshops that we liked the best was the notion of "Who's that smile?" The visual would be close-ups on celebrities with distinctive mouths who have used BriteSmile. (Think Jack Nicholson, Angelina Jolie, Bette Midler, or the one we chose to use, Jim Carrey.) The fun would be in guessing who the smile belongs to, without having to guess too hard.

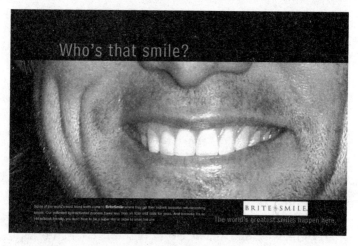

Who's that smile?

BRITE☆SMILE.
The world's greatest smiles happen here.

Celebrity smiles speak volumes.

One major hurdle with celebrity endorsements—you've got to get the celebrities to do it. So let's try the same idea without celebrities. And let's hope we don't end up with green lips or a rippled tongue.

The most obvious (and probably lazy) thing to do is to try replacing the celebrity smile with a Joe Schmo smile. Doesn't work because frankly, who cares whose smile it is if they're not famous? So there's got to be something else. The hard part is how do you create a campaign based on smiles and teeth and whitening that doesn't look like all the rest? Do we put the BriteSmile logo on the teeth like we put the lotion logo on the skin? Create a signature "sparkle" that is a result of our process? Or is there something in the quality or character of the smile itself that might say even more?

The answer to this came out of our favorite "take a picture of yourself" exercise in the workshops, where we pass around a camera and have everyone, well, take a picture of him- or herself. Since this was about noncelebrity smiles, we wanted noncelebrity inspiration. We told them that their picture was going to be part of an enduring campaign that featured real people's smiles that were beautiful and white but in a less typical fashion. In a way, this was the anticelebrity brand. They had to come up with the set of words that would be the enduring tagline for this series of imperfectly attractive smiles. Imagine what your answer would have been before you read on.

smiles we love.

Rachel Jennings
Atlanta, Ga

BriteSmile.

BRITE·SMILE.
LOVE YOUR SMILE.

Love Your Smile: Our noncelebrity campaign.

As you can see, we also mixed the first- and second-person voice in this concept, saying that these are "Smiles we love" but that you, too, can "Love your smile." This one reminds me of Dove's "campaign for real beauty." I think the down-to-earth, real-people imagery works much better with the Dove brand than with BriteSmile. Dove is less expensive and their everyday appeal matches the everyday use of their products. For a high-price, premium product, the celebrity endorsement fits far better.

This kind of Monday morning quarterbacking is easy

to do only because we are doing it in retrospect. If you never push your ideas this far out, you will never know which ones are going to work best for your brand.

The Two-Word Drill
Finding two words that last more than two years could be the hardest thing you do

If the nineties were filled with Nike copycats trying to write their own three-word phenomenon, these days it's all about the two-word drill. Yes, we've reduced the brilliant slogan word count by 50 percent.

> *Live richly.*
> *Think different.*
> *Drivers wanted.*

Even "Got Milk?" for that matter. Some of the most successful pioneers of our day got their brand out loud and clear with just two words. And unlike the dearth of present participle and first person taglines, there is no shortage of two-word taglines in today's brand sphere.

> *Higher Standards.*
> *Ask Merrill.*
> *Never follow.*

Do more.
Beyond petroleum.
Pure Life.
Changes everything.
Intel inside.
Everyone's invited.

With such a list, you'd think that maybe you'd want to overturn the brandwagon and be the first with a twenty-word tagline instead. And maybe there's reason in that, but there's an even bigger reason why two-word taglines work: They're small and they pack a punch. It's the extra-strength, concentrated version of a brand message, and you get to finish your whole thought before your audience has a chance to stop listening.

But how to create these two-worded branding gems? Should it include the product name, such as "Ask Merrill" or "Intel inside"? Should it be a call to action, such as "Do more" or "Think different"? Again, the only way to find out is to play around a little.

Think about other things that typically use two words as part of their normal syntax: signage (Exit Only), advanced praise for movies ("Utterly unforgettable!"), or my brainstorming favorite, the work of art. The reason this exercise works so well is because it allows you to create the visual, and then name it afterward as if it were hanging in a museum or gallery. You can evoke different styles, different artists, and different media to create different two-word combinations, as long as it's not *Untitled 2006*.

Let's pretend first that Norman Rockwell was going to paint a modern Americana picture of the BriteSmile experience. What do you imagine the scene to be? Knowing that BriteSmile spas are less clinical, more spalike than a regular dentists' office, does that change your answer? Think about it. (My painting: a woman in a spalike environment with her mouth being worked on. My title: Say Aaahh.) What if Andy Warhol was going to do a painting? How does that affect not only the visual, but the two words you use to describe it? (My painting: four mimeographed smiles, but all in different shades of white. My title: Technicolor White.) Or is there a better candidate than either of those?

This exercise for us unearthed two very interesting elements, only one of them being the two-word tagline, "Simply Brilliant." The other element was the notion of "The Art of the Smile." While the idea was that we treated whitening as a true art form and that all of our works of art would be in white, I don't think we did it justice in this iteration. (I blame the word "introduces.")

BriteSmile introduces The Art of the Smile.

Some even whitening go it provides, but we see it as an art. Come to BriteSmile and see how easy you can love your teeth in just one hour, in just one hour.

BRITE★SMILE.
Simply brilliant.

Simply Brilliant: The two words were good, the rest . . . eh.

Sometimes, we have a vision of an idea and once we develop it the client changes his or her mind. This time, they were right. The client never liked this idea, they let us develop it anyway, and then it bombed instantly upon presentation. Again, it brings me back to the point that you have to try a few different things to see which ones fit better than others. As Austin Powers would say, "The two-word drill is totally not my bag, baby." But I never would have known it until I tried.

From "Wow!" to "What is this?"

Ten ways to ruin a perfectly good branding concept

Colin Wheildon, author of *Type and Layout* includes a piece called "Eight Ways to Ruin a Perfectly Good Ad." The first time I read it I thought it was a brilliant idea, and I must not have been the first. Within a few minutes on Google, I unearthed "Eight Ways to Ruin a Perfectly Good Story," "Eight Ways to Ruin a Perfectly Good Sales Force," "Eight Ways to Ruin a Perfectly Good Marriage," and "Eight Ways to Ruin a Perfectly Good [Gaming] Format." I have decided to include my own "eight ways," plus two more for good measure. Here are my "Eight Ways to Ruin a Perfectly Good Branding Concept, plus two."

1. *Make the visual smaller and the product bigger*

Why? Why? Why do people relegate the picture to less than one quarter of the page? This is your imagery. This is your promise. People have seen a picture of a plastic bottle, a bag of chips, a toothpaste tube, and a cereal box before. If your product has a specific feature that you need to convey clearly, then go ahead. Just don't make everyday objects into heroes on the page. The argument we get on this issue (and most of the others on this list) is: "Hey, it's our product and that's what people are going to see first on the shelves, so this will mirror the marketplace." Hello!? If it were the marketplace, your consumer wouldn't be sitting in a focus group, eating free pretzels or answering an online survey and reacting to bullet points about your product.

2. *Capitalize The First Letter Of Every Word In A Sentence*

There is no better way to make your thoughts more awkward and less readable than doing this. A few exceptions to this rule: If your headline or tagline is a real, authoritative statement (e.g., The Ultimate Driving Machine), is part of an anagram (ABC. American Broadcasting Company), or sounds like the title of a book (The Listening Bank). The more you can make concept headlines and taglines look like real people talk, the easier it will be for real people to read it.

3. *Put it in "quotation marks"*

If you want to convey that a person is talking, by all means go ahead and slap on some quotation marks. But *never* put your tagline in quotation marks just so people know it's a tagline: "Your City Plumbers" or "A Cut Above the Rest." (For some reason lots of contractors and hair salons fall victim to this mode.) Worse yet, include some kind of double entendre or pun in your tagline and put the quotation marks around it so that you know everyone gets the punch line, such as: We "sink" the competition or "Hair" today, "hair" tomorrow.

4. *Shove in as much information as possible*

Following is a real excerpt a client gave me from the guidelines for how to write concepts.

The headline:
- should be an attention getter
- includes the name of the brand/product
- introduces the product
- captures the essence of the concept (primary and secondary benefit)
- is concise

Main text:
- gives reasons why the consumers should care (primary and secondary benefits, reassurances)
- conveys what the consumer would learn from advertising and at the shelf
- describes how they are to use the product, when and why (if unclear)
- includes a frame of reference so consumers know where product fits
- contains one to three messages, but fewer is better (depends on category and importance of education)
- if new product, says so

No wonder these concepts are so unreadable. But how much explaining should one concept need? Either consumers get it or they don't. The more you have to explain it, the less it seems like you know what you're selling.

5. *Say the same thing over and over*

Nothing is worse than reading on and on about one particular thing. It gets to the point when after a few sentences you stop paying attention. And yet the concept still goes on. Way longer than you wanted it to go on in the first place. It goes on about many different points, which say related things in different ways. Just when you think it might end, it just keeps going. And you want it to stop but it doesn't. Just says the same thing over and over again. But in different ways and using different adjectives.

6. *Make it into a "mood board"*

A mood board is a collage of twenty or so pictures that are supposed to represent the "mood" of a brand. To me they look like some project a kid makes for art class. The more you see them, the worse they appear to get. If you can't get your brand message across using one good visual, twenty mediocre ones—whether you selected them or your consumers did—aren't going to do the trick. This is branding, not arts and crafts.

7. *Mention the product name at least three times in copy and once more with tagline*

Sure, it's good to test for memorability and name acceptance, but after three times in the body copy and then again with the oversized picture of the product, it just makes the syntax—and those trying to read it—uncomfortable. Imagine you're looking at a concept for Flakey Flakes. You've already seen the name a few times in the body copy and then you look at the product before reading the tagline. This is how your consumer's mind is hearing it: "[On package: Flakey Flakes.] Flakey Flakes. The flakiest flakes you can get." In the marketplace you typically see a logo or product with a sign-off that doesn't repeat the name. Now you can see the reason for it.

8. *Use the same font for each concept*

"We want to standardize our concepts!" marketers cry. This is the most confusing and contradictive statement. The same people who insist that the product must be big to reflect marketplace reality want to strip it of the realistic look and feel that different fonts and designs might add to the product. It overlooks the importance of having visual and verbal cues that work together. Remember: What you say is just as important as how you say it. Or to paraphrase Billy Crystal, "It's not how you sound, but how you look."

9. *Use line art instead of a real picture*

Line art is the death of a good product. It automatically signals to your audience that the product is not real. What if you don't have a real product? Take a picture of a similar product with a white label on it and stick your name on there. Ask someone who knows Photoshop to doctor the hell out of it. Even basic Word drawing programs or digital camera software can help you manipulate photos. If you can put together a Power Point presentation with a soundtrack and moving slides, you should be able to do this.

10. *Bullet points*

Nothing says consumer *un*friendly like a few bullet points in the middle of your body copy. You want the consumers to understand the attributes and benefits of your brand, but there's got to be a better way. Maybe if there weren't so many attributes and benefits in each concept, you wouldn't need bullet points in the first place.

5

Passing a Buck Can Go a Long, Long Way

Making creative people create

Up until a few years ago, my most creatively daunting projects were those that involved either a product that wasn't very good or one that relied on pure imagery. The challenge was always in thinking about a nonrational idea in a rational way. For example, the idea of branding bottled water. I used to say that if you could brand water—a clear, tasteless beverage available for free in every home in most parts of the world—you could brand anything. Even harder? Financial products and services. These intangibles don't even have the luxury that bottled water and other consumer package goods have of being some-thing you could touch, see, and smell.

And then we were given an assignment so challeng-ing, it made branding financial services seem like the eas-iest thing in the world. The consumer marketing group at Time Inc. had already hired us five times for projects in-volving their major publications, including *Entertainment Weekly, People, Time, Fortune,* and *Sports Illustrated.* Each project dealt with different business objectives, from in-creasing gift subscriptions, suggesting new co-branding opportunities, and even discovering a premium that could outdo the popularity of the infamous sneaker phone. After a number of projects, they saw how our process could adapt to any project—from naming to branding to new products. So it was project number six that became the big bad tough assignment: They wanted to apply the Brandmaker Express process to help them create a "cul-ture of innovation" (their exact words) in their corporate workplace. At first, I wasn't sure how to approach it—essentially I was being asked to create concepts that would help them coach people into being creative who are already creative for a living. (Talk about intangible!) They publish magazines and create news daily. These are usu-ally the people we look to for leading the trends and now they were looking to us. Is this branding? Did they want a human resources initiative, a shrink, or a brand expert? I wasn't sure, and it gave me pause.

But not enough pause to say no.

It was branding, in fact, and the more I thought about it the more clear it became. The task was to create new products, new initiatives, and relevant names that made those initiatives meaningful. What was unique to this project was that it turned creativity into a commodity. Instead of figuring out how to get Pam from Peoria to want our new flavor of corn flakes, we had to make Sam from the sales department want to create more ideas. Putting it in this frame made the task, if nothing else, less intimidating. I mean, Time Inc. is so innovative on their own (their corporate Web site asserts: "Innovation has been a key to Time Inc.'s success"), making them even more innovative was a huge (and somewhat amorphous) responsibility. And so Joe and I proceeded to approach it as we would any other project. We also based a lot of our thinking on our own process and, specifically, what we do in the workshops that helps our participants be more creative—which is why I am including it in this book. If it works for us, surely it can work for others.

It was time to put the process to the test.

Negating the Negative
Turning obstacles into opportunities

It may sound counterintuitive, but one of the best places to start looking for a compelling branding message or new product is in the last place you'd think to look. Negatives have a way of identifying the points of resistance that your audience has, and therefore gives you several opportunities to address them and resolve them head-on. What are some examples? Maybe you have a bad value proposition, your product is outdated, or your new cheese pocket can sit on the shelves for well into the next decade. Or in this case, we needed to identify the elements of their corporate culture that were uncreative to start out with.

During the briefing we invited the client to tell us why our corporate culture doesn't stand a chance of inspiring creativity of any kind. The list of negatives was not surprising. Among them were:

> *not enough time/too busy*
> *there's nothing new*
> *environment too corporate*
> *why should I?*

Sound familiar? Yes, every marketer thinks he or she has the tallest hurdles ("My market is so saturated!" "My product is a low-interest commodity." "Been there. Tried that. Didn't work. Got the T-shirt.") And yet the tendency is to run away from these obstacles instead of addressing them.

Now it's not enough just to be negative. The point is

to create a positive solution to each particular negative. This last sentence unfortunately reminds me of this ridiculous training manual I read while working at a restaurant chain, with rules such as "Turn a complaint into a compliment" and "Smile. And don't forget to look natural." What makes our version less patronizing and more productive is that we're not ignoring the negative—we're using it to our advantage.

In a product branding or positioning challenge, we would take any of those drawbacks and imagine that a consumer is actually confronting you with it. (In this case, the employees are the consumers.) As any good salesman would (and remember, the essence of branding is selling), we have to offer something that will overcome their objection and make their gripe nonexistent. It's amazing what happens when you address a specific problem. All of a sudden, you can imagine solutions, products, and compelling messages simply by tapping into your own tools of persuasion.

Here are those same negatives with a potential solution attached:

> *not enough time/too busy*—create specific "creative times"
> *there's nothing new*—maybe look at old ideas
> *environment too corporate*—make surroundings more creative

why should I?—give people incentives to do the work

From these four negatives came four very different ideas about what we could do to make the culture more innovative. We used these as a basis for some of the exercises for the workshops. This is where the discipline of the workshops pays off. Instead of just being happy uncovering certain possible solution areas, we want to solve them completely. In developing exercises for the format, we make sure that each one has two very specific components. The first component must be the consumer insight, strategic direction, or marketing possibility. And each exercise also must foment some inspiration that will have participants thinking less pragmatically and more innovatively.

Too many times, brainstorming efforts are either very tactical—"What is the new package we should create?"—or too obtuse—"Think about how you would stick a straw in a potato." By using a balance of real hypotheses with forward-thinking tactics, we elicit answers that are fresh as well as feasible.

So let's take a look at some of those negatives-turned-positives, and see what happens with a little brain input.

The 25-Hour Day Meets Miller Time
Who's got time to be creative?

Everyone is busy these days. Type As rule the office space, and the harder you work, the more is expected of you. New products and services sprout up every day promising to get things done quicker, faster, or easier so that you can have more time to relax, get back to work, see your kids, or do anything besides what they're selling.

Being crazed, especially at work, is nothing new. You've heard the old complaint about needing more hours in the day to get things done. But until our planet alters its rotational time frame, what we really need to focus on is how to make busy people (more specifically, the busy people at Time Inc.) find more time to be creative.

To do that, there was an exercise in the workshops where we passed out a copied page from a day planner and asked every person to mark down his or her most creative time throughout the workday. The time could be an actual hour, a general time ("between meetings"), a mental time ("when I'm relaxed"), or any kind of time they wanted. If Miller beer could own the "Miller Time" state of mind, perhaps it could work for us. By keeping the possibilities open, we're also allowing for the greatest variety of ideas within a certain exercise. Everyone interprets exercises differently, and sometimes that can be a good thing. Before reading on, ask yourself when your creative time would be.

After identifying a specific time, participants then had to come up with a name for a time-based program inspired by the time frame they chose. The reason that we asked for the name only is that we wanted the ideas to be short and concise. A name forces the idea into its most pure form. The winning idea came from a woman who explained that she always came into work a half-hour early to get things done before everyone else got into work. She called her program The Early Bird. Being a big morning fan, I instantly warmed to this idea. I could readily visualize a meeting or work session that started a half-hour before the standard workday. But how to get people to show up?

That would be easy. Free food motivates people like nothing I've ever seen. I am convinced that when company associates agree to attend our three-hour brainstorming meeting (not knowing that prizes and fun will ensue), at least half come just for the free grub. Not that I mind. Sipping a cup of coffee and munching on a bagel not only makes work more enjoyable, it fuels your body with creative energy. Borrowing from the success of attendance at the brainstorming sessions, the Early-Bird concept featured free food front and center for our communication, so we named it The Breakfast Club.

Like many—if not most—of my clients who do not run television or print ads for their products, this program and others would be promoted via e-mail, flyers, and perhaps some other internal communications. Then why present

The Breakfast Club: A panini for your thoughts

the idea this way if it doesn't beget an ad campaign? Because it's essential to find and communicate the key hot button or buttons, in this case being early morning and free food. According to this concept, The Breakfast Club would meet once a month for half an hour—volunteers only. The participants would have only thirty minutes to solve a particular challenge (remember, the deadline is your friend). Time Consumer Marketing could either hold the meeting before the workday started, or start on time and let people get to their desks thirty minutes late. When you think about the value of collective, focused, and voluntary brainpower, having a few tardy employees isn't such a huge sacrifice after all.

This was one of the ideas that didn't immediately rise to the top. When I asked our client if she had ever implemented this idea, she said that she hadn't, but now that I had brought it up she forgot why she hadn't and would give it another look. Looks like even food for thought needs a little, well, stirring up every once in a while.

Behold the Business Card
Capturing the entrepreneurial spirit

We hear plenty of bad ideas in a workshop. Quite often, a participant will volunteer a name that's already taken by a competitor (a new Centrum vitamin called One-a-Day), other times a new product idea is totally "out-there" ("they should have an edible can"), and sometimes rally cries and taglines are accidentally inappropriate ("Jerk yourself back into health"). However, just because an idea got expressed in a bad way doesn't mean the idea is bad. The same thing goes for those old ideas that never work, but never die. Why not give bad ideas another chance with a little refinement or rethinking? Centrum could surely come up with a line of products for different daily needs, or even preempt a time-release twenty-four-hour claim. Aluminum cans might not be edible, but maybe your new product features an edible spoon or is positioned as a "mess-less" meal. And while the terminology isn't right, the notion of making a "comeback" or a "return to wellness" is a great way to make a health claim. The lessons here are that most bad ideas have something good about them, and a little tweaking can go a long way.

That's why in our workshops ideas become a real commodity. We let people pour out as many ideas as possible, and look for the good in every one. It allows people to volunteer good ideas, bad ideas, ideas that failed—even ideas that don't make any sense initially. We collect these ideas during the workshops and do the tweaking later.

Translating that to this project, all we needed to do was to create a place, most likely an intranet Web site, at Time Inc. where employees could submit and collect ideas and see what was salvageable in any of them. One person's idea trash may be another's business treasure. What was missing was the right kind of imagery that would take an idea depository and turn it into a brand.

We handed out blank business cards to all the participants in the workshop and told them they had quit their jobs at Time Inc. because they had started this great new idea-collecting business they opened up in a local strip mall. They had to tell us the name of their business and their company's rally cry. Here's your blank business card. Name your idea-collecting endeavor. Trust me, it's only daunting for the first minute or so.

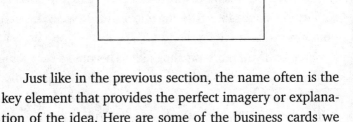

Just like in the previous section, the name often is the key element that provides the perfect imagery or explanation of the idea. Here are some of the business cards we saw:

The Idea Library
Find your answer here

Idea Mates
Where people and ideas find each other

The Idea Bank
An answer for every challenge

The Loser's Lounge
For underappreciated genius

From the resource-driven Idea Library to the tongue-in-cheek Loser's Lounge, these are four totally different business names with four distinctly different personalities. The one we chose to develop, however, was called The Recycle Bin. We loved the thought of recycling ideas and the efficiency, smartness, and do-gooder imagery that recycling already evokes. Also, the imagery cultivated the kind of idea sharing and reusing that saves corporations a whole lot of time and money (not unlike recycling). Reduce, Reuse, Recycle. For our purposes, we changed that well-known trilogy to: Recall, Resubmit, Reward.

The Recycle Bin: 100 percent reusable ideas.

To the best of my knowledge, this idea still rests ironically in its own unacknowledged recycle bin. But maybe someday it will get a second chance.

Why the reward? Because in nearly any situation where you are asking people to go above and beyond their regular job duties, it helps to have an incentive of sorts and the marketing group was willing to put some money behind this initiative. The reward does not have to be monetary. It can be physical, mental, or spiritual. But more on that later. What The Recycle Bin created for Time Consumer Marketing was not only a forum where the right idea might come into its own but also a place where employees could purge themselves of their pet ideas and perhaps make room for some new ones.

Changing Atmospheric Conditions
Creating the New Casual Friday

I remember going to meet with clients on a Friday and we would be dressed in our best business suits and they would be wearing khakis and logo-embroidered polo shirts. They would look at us with pity and make some comment along the lines of "Oh, too bad you didn't know it was casual today!" (Of course, as a consultant who was working from home most days, every day was casual day. The only days when I'd have to even change out of my sweats was when I was meeting with one of those clients.) This was at the height of casual Fridays when you could sense a noticeable difference in the attitude and atmosphere of a corporation because people got to feel more comfortable. Now that every day is casual day in most companies, the initial effect of going casual has worn off. (Some companies have actually reinstated their dress codes, which is an interesting turn of events.) But there was something in the idea of those casual Fridays that did work—at least for a while—and it was that thinking that inspired our next exercise.

We said that instead of casual Friday, something really special happens on one Friday a month. Something that made them feel more inspired and more creative.

What was it?

Some of the ideas we got back were a touch too hokey, such as dress-up days (think costume party meets corporate headquarters); too uncorporate, such as "wear-your-pajamas-to-work" days (a waking nightmare?); or just too unappealing, such as Barefoot Fridays (let's not go there). That's okay because there were three great ideas that did come from this exercise.

The first idea was simple—offer field trips once a month to different places. It could be anywhere from a department store to a bowling alley, but each field trip would come with a business objective that needed to be solved by something inspired by that place. In truth, we do a lot of store wandering in our creative work, and we also find ourselves mentally solution-hunting whether we're at the gym or on a plane. In that sense, offering a series of field trips seemed like a logical idea. My favorite part of this concept, and what I feel gives it such a compelling brand, is the name: Mystery Bus Trips. Even if you only went around the block, it would feel like an adventure.

The second idea that came from this exercise was actually a perfect example of a bad-idea-gone-good. We always say in the workshops that there are no bad ideas, a blatant lie that everyone understands, but always with the

Mystery Bus Trips: This bus is filled with the team from Time.

clarification that some of the most preposterous, out-there responses have led us to some very original and meaningful ideas. One of the worst ideas, I believe, was to have theme days at the office, where everyone had to dress according to a certain—and seemingly irrelevant—theme. This sounds like one of those incredibly wasteful exercises in creative futility. And to have to do it monthly? Talk about having a time of the month that makes you crabby. However, using creative themes to solve unrelated business challenges . . . that sounds painless enough. And so we created theme months minus the dress-up factor, and the Monthly Mind Openers were born. This was as simple as introducing a unique theme that might help people solve a creative challenge by approaching it in a new way. Monthly themes could be anything: colors, geographies, objects, moods, sports, etc. Every month employees would either solve a specific business objective provided by the marketing group or be asked to reexamine some of their own challenges using the inspiration of that month's theme.

The third one was by far my favorite because it took the wisdom of casual Friday to the next level and simultaneously addressed the overscheduling of meetings and mandatory events within a corporation. Essentially, once a month there would be a day where you couldn't schedule any meetings or mandatory events so that people could have the whole day to do just what they wanted.

Free-Form Fridays: Barefoot in spirit only, of course.

Imagine a whole day to sit at your desk, uninterrupted time to work on the things you don't get to work on within a normal workday. It's a vacation from work without leaving the building.

What Would The Donald Do?
Creating the corporate reality TV show

When we first started our business, we didn't offer rewards during the workshops. Instead, we used a different prop for each exercise to help participants focus in on one thought or element, similar to the Monthly Mind Openers. We would bring in Mickey Mouse ears when we wanted people to think "magical," chef's hats when we wanted delicious descriptions, batteries when we wanted people to think about energy. The most popular exercise and the one that made people focus the most and work the hardest was the one we called The Dollar Exercise. Every participant was handed a dollar bill with a Post-It note attached. Whoever had the best answer (chosen by us, somewhat arbitrarily) would keep all the money. We always saved this prop for the most difficult question, because the dollars became such incredible motivators. It's amazing how seriously people will approach a problem when there's twelve dollars at stake. It took us a while to catch on, but it dawned on us that offering a prize might be better than just showing a prop. So after that, a few exercises featured rewards. If we were invoking Calvin Klein, we would have a CK perfume reward. The prize for the billboard exercise might be a keychain or car-related reward. Each time there was some prize, the quality and the focus of the responses improved greatly. Not long after, we offered a reward for the "best answer" for every exercise. As time went on, we realized that it wasn't the prize itself that mattered so much as the notion that there was a reward to be had. And a little friendly competition didn't seem to hurt either.

Rewards, competition, challenges . . . sounds kind of like reality television, doesn't it?

I confess, I am a reality show junkie. There is something so compelling to me about watching absolute strangers vie for love, money, fame, recognition—or all four. One of my favorite shows of this highly "intellectual" television genre is *The Apprentice* (and not just because Randal, a classmate of mine from high school actually won in season four).

What makes reality television such a rich source of inspiration for new business programs, promotions, and other service initiatives is the infinite permutations (or just mutations) of the basic reality TV premise: Make it a competition and they will come.

So imagine that the producer, Mark Burnett, gives you a call and tells you that he has created the next great reality show where contestants are forced to find innovative ways to solve specific business challenges. How do you think he did it? Was it like *The Apprentice* with large teams who slowly shrink down to one winner? Or like *Fear Factor* with individual players and multiple challenges? How long did the competition last? How big was the reward? And what was the name of your program?

This one creative exercise created innovation programs that even a nonreality TV lover would love.

One person named his program after the actual television program *Mission Impossible*. His show used the imagery and the fun of the spy missions as a way to make some of the business challenges that would be featured interesting. Each week there would be a different business mission left in a briefcase by the elevator. The focus of the weekly business missions could be on anything and everything. As you can see, we loved the imagery it evoked and ran with it in this concept.

If you choose to accept this challenge, you may be greatly rewarded.

Dare to take on the impossible.

Mission Impossible

Mission Impossible: A little imagery goes a long way.

The marketing group at Time Inc. has implemented Mission Impossible several times. For the first few times, it even had someone standing at the elevator in a trench coat and fedora handing out the ideas to go with the concept. Since this initiative elicited so many ideas, the prizes were chosen at random and the winning ideas were posted on the company intranet.

Another person came up with a show inspired by *The Amazing Race* called The Idea Slam, where small teams would have two weeks to solve one major business crisis. We loved this idea since it incorporated two major elements of our own creative process: It featured a set deadline and it focused the thinking around one major challenge at a time. What made this idea even better was that each team would present their ideas in an auditorium, which made it almost like the best of reality television without the commercials. It inspired even those who weren't participating to witness the action, and let those who competed share the spotlight and be in the public eye.

The other winning element of this idea was the big prize purse that they offered to the winning team. While small prizes can motivate a room full of people, large prizes show that ideas have true value and are not the commodity that everyone thinks.

To date, this has been the most successful and most

often-repeated program for our clients at Time Inc. They just ran their third Idea Slam not long before this was written and other divisions within the building have heard of its success and begun to use it too. There are never a lack of applicants and the ten teams of ten people always fill up within a day or two of announcing the event. Our client tells me that this idea more than any other works so well specifically because the restricted time frame gives it such high energy. Plus, it has worked to create a real sense of community, and has given the Time Consumer Marketing group the bragging rights within Time Inc. as the pioneer of this often-replicated program. Most important, it has been a valuable resource for successful business innovations. Even ideas that did not win the contest are currently being developed.

There was one last concept inspired by reality television (my favorite show, in fact) that was not as successful, but no less brilliant, called Venture Capital. Like the Idea Slam, this idea was looking for quality over quantity, but the reward was pure genius. Basically, teams would work together to create a new business plan of their choice based on a certain amount of capital that would be the prize. In the case of Time Inc., the plan could be for a new magazine, a new subscription model, a new co-branding partner, or anything revenue building. Teams would present their idea to top management, who would then reward their favorite (and most lucrative) plan by investing the prize money in its development.

Think about the beauty of this—using company money to inspire company employees to create a lucrative business plan for the company. Simple, isn't it? And it's cheaper than hiring a consultant and much more motivational to boot. It inspired employees to be entrepreneurs. And the prize for the participants could be a percentage of the venture money, a business-related reward such as a PDA or Blackberry, or even a chance to further develop the business (let's hear it for creating your own destiny!).

However good an idea I thought this was, it never "out-Trumped" the Idea Slam. Perhaps Mark Burnett could use a new TV reality show.

The Time Inc. Takeaway
What's in it for you?

More than in any other project, the employees of the Time Consumer Marketing group—executives and assistants alike—created nearly all of the winning concepts and ideas during the creative workshops we ran. Once we inspired the thinking, they were off and running in no time. And I believe the same thing happened once our concepts were delivered to them. They used some concepts very literally, and others they used as springboards for other initiatives they ran. Our client admitted that—years later—she still has the boards right next to her desk and references them when she's looking for new and fresh ways to keep their culture of innovation going strong.

Inspiring creativity is one of the toughest challenges any good brand builder can face. Brainstorming—whether it be with twenty people or just two—should be focused, fun, and productive in order to get the best results. The reason I mention that here is because creating a culture of innovation for Time Consumer Marketing was akin to taking what works in workshops and applying it on a broader scale. If creativity can be a commodity, then here are some guidelines that will ensure a wealth of ideas:

1. *Bad ideas become good ones*

What makes really bad ideas so bad is that they stand out from the ones that are safe, familiar, normal. Remember how much J-Lo's dress stood out at the Oscars? Some would say it's a bad dress, and yet that's the dress we remember. Bad ideas stand out because they're unfamiliar, unexpected, and lots of times, unordinary. And those are the kinds of things you should pay attention to when they pop up on your bad-idea radar screen. When you shut out the bad ideas, you also keep the good ones from coming in.

2. *Make sure everyone speaks up, even the shy sorts*

Have you ever noticed that in a couple there is often one who is talkative and one who is quiet? I always gravitate to the more outgoing, talkative one, only to find out in time that the shy one has a lot more to say. I'm not sure if it's because talking less gives them more time to think, to observe, to meditate, or what; but I feel like I would have really missed out by not getting to know them better. When hunting for creativity, make sure you have a venue that encourages those who stay in the background to have their voice heard. In other words, don't forget to water your wallflowers.

3. *Steal heavily from the crap on TV*

On television they have contestants doing stuff you'd never think they would. If someone will munch a maggot for a small chance at stardom, what makes you think that your employees couldn't use a healthy dose of friendly creative competition? And if you think reality TV is the only inspiration, grab your remote control and start flipping. With 150 channels of game shows, soap operas, news programs, makeover shows, talk shows, sportscasts, documentaries, and shopping networks, it's never been easier to turn garbage into gold.

4. *Dangle the cubic zirconia*

Incentive bonuses that are essentially cheap become incredibly meaningful. Don't ask me why, they just do. A friend of mine is a pretty good ex-junior high school bowler who averaged in the 170s as a fourteen-year-old and now bowls about once every five years. One of these times he found out they were giving out a real bowling pin to the winner, and his competitive bowler of years gone by was resurrected. He got four strikes in a row in the final game to take home the pin. (Remember: This is a grown man working his ass off for a bowling pin.) Without the incentive, he would've concentrated on eating the chicken wings and drinking beer like everyone else.

5. *Set the stopwatch*

By putting the pressure on people to become creative in a short amount of time, you're making them more creative. A scientist once told me it was sometimes easier to be creative in between filling out grant applications than it was when he had a job where he was hired to be creative forty hours a week. He felt nobody is that good, and limited time is a great motivator.

6. *One bite at a time*

There's nothing worse than having to come up with a finished idea all at once. It's way too daunting and most
great ideas are built, not born. By asking for one element
of an idea at a time (the name, the mechanics, the payoff,
the promise), you will automatically get clues on how to
make the idea whole.

7. *Not all group-think should be done by a group*

Have you ever been trying to think of one song while
another is playing on the radio? This is often what happens when all the thinking in a brainstorming session is
all participation all the time. It's better to give each person
a chance to have a few seconds to think independently
on what his or her answer would be. In other words, let
them whistle their own tune first before everyone
chimes in.

8. *Try moving sideways*

When sparring in karate, I have a tendency to walk
straight in to try to land a strike or kick on my opponent.
Almost always I get hit first. "Try moving sideways" I hear
being yelled from the sidelines by my karate master. Same

thing with solving problems creatively. Seeing your goal and making a beeline for it is not always the smartest path. The trick is to find unrelated inspiration that's not necessarily irrelevant.

9. *Let's put on a show*

Who doesn't love a talent show? Reverting to the old summer-camp showcase gets everyone involved, whether you're a participant or a viewer. In fact, summer-camp rosters were full of activities designed for group participation, creative expression, and team building exercises. Short of building a campfire in the next cubicle and singing "Kum-ba-ya," think about other ways to make creative times more fun and inclusive.

10. *Fill out a restraining order*

On my college entrance application, I had to write an essay on a quotation that read: "The wise restraints that make men free." At the time, I probably wrote something relatively juvenile and clichéd about how people need to learn the foundations of a craft before expressing themselves creatively (e.g., writers need to understand the rules of grammar and spelling before they write poetry;

musicians need to practice basic chords before participating in an impromptu jam session). My response now would be much different. It would be that creativity loves discipline. The mind flourishes when given a specific task instead of an open-ended one.

Branded It Myself

Oy Vey! Can It be Done?

My parents Googled me a while ago and discovered that I had done pro bono branding work with a New York City–based Jewish nonprofit organization called Aish NY. It probably gave them a little bit of joy to know that their hopelessly secular daughter participated in the Jewish community at a time other than the High Holidays. I agreed to do the work mostly because I like feeling like a do-gooder, partially because I have the guilt of being a "bad Jew," and also because I was hoping to grab the attention of some of Aish's high-power contributors and members, including Kenneth Cole, Kurt Douglas, and Steven Spielberg.

Doing a free job meant that I had to make some adjustments in how I approached this project. I couldn't pay honoraria to have help at the workshops, I couldn't dedicate the normal amount of mental time and energy because I had other paid projects going on, and I didn't want to ask our other employees to also give their time for my personal volunteer efforts.

I had completed the Brandmaker Express process hundreds of times, but I was put in a position to test drive our model all on my own. The normal give and take of our brainstorming sessions would now give way to my entirely internal dialogues. That is, me talking (and fretting) to myself.

The Challenge

Aish New York's West-Coast cousin, Aish Los Angeles, claims the proud title of the Originators of Speed Dating. For the as-of-yet uninitiated, Speed Dating entails a series of seven seven-minute dates (a kindred believer in the power of quick thinking). And although high-intensity dating is a big draw for Aish, they also offer other more subtle ways of meeting friends and potential Jewish mates, such as trips, events, lectures, and parties. As the buzzword of branding passed from the mouths of businessmen to the ears of the leadership there, the folks at Aish began to wonder if they too needed to develop a brand that could set them apart from a dozen other competitors.

What distinguished Aish from the pack was its philosophy and approach, which was very thoughtful and less orthodox (in every sense of the word) than some of the other associations, even though many of its leaders and members were orthodox Jews. Most notably, it knew that it wanted its brand to attract the secular skeptics and observant Jews alike. Whatever I created would have to talk to both audiences.

But was this dual-audience approach a wise one?

I am surely not conveying any kind of marketing breakthrough by saying it's not usually a good idea to go after two very different audiences at the same time. Which is why one of the things that I really wanted to play with, explore, push, pull, and stretch, were separate and distinct personalities that represented varying degrees of traditional and nontraditional Judaism. Only after I did that, we could see if there would—or should—be any middle ground.

Finding Opportunities

Following the briefing with Aish, I did what I always do: Look back at my notes and create an outline of ideas. Remember, these are one, two, or three words that encapsulate challenges, obstacles, hypotheses, or anything else that sticks out in my mind. Unlike regular notes, I recommend that each key point should be written out on its own line, so it reads more like a list than anything else. It's as easy, well, as making a list, but—as you've learned in previous chapters—what I'm really doing is putting the creative process in motion. I'm identifying jumping-off points, potential strategies, and helping identify separate and distinct single-minded brand areas. Here are some of the comments from my notes in this format:

> *meeting people and making a connection is one of the key drivers of membership*
> *the brand must come across as Jewish*
> *no one knows what Aish means*
> *the events and programs are contemporary and sometimes controversial*
> *urban/hip/modern*
> *people have negative preconceptions about what a Jewish association would be*
> *make it fun*
> *address the skeptics*
> *use Jewish words in a cool way*

In my business life, I would take each one of these ideas and create a workshop exercise that might help others to build on each idea. But with no workshops and no "others," was it worth the effort? Or was there a different way to approach it? The answer is twofold. I could immediately visualize potential creative answers to some of these ideas, but others were not as apparent. So I took the spirit of a workshop and did it more informally.

Creating My Own Creative Team
The informal brainstorming session

I have a good friend named Roger, whom I love joking around with. He's one of those guys whom I can say something to and he builds on it, and it goes back and forth like a creative tennis match. He's Jewish, to boot, so it's no surprise that I called him to join me in some informal brainstorming. We met for a beer and some chicken wings, and I asked him to help me out. You can ask anyone you know to be a good sounding board, a proficient idea builder, a far-out thinker, or any combination thereof.

Not unlike a real workshop, I wanted to make sure that we stayed within the boundaries of what kind of answers I was looking for. So I explained that I was having trouble thinking of taglines that would include Jewish words in a cool, hip way. My example of this was the word "kosher," which I've heard people use in place of "cool" or "truthful" or "everything's okay." The reason I was stuck on this word was because it had crept into secular society and had taken on a somewhat universal meaning, whether a friend warned you that the guy you met last weekend was "not entirely kosher" or reassured you that "that's okay, it's kosher, dude" concerning potential doubt.

So first we compiled some taglines that featured kosher and its permutations:

> *100 percent Kosher*
> *98% Kosher (inviting the skeptics in)*
> *The Kosher Counterculture*

These taglines were, as my grandmother would say, "Feh." But what other words were there that said Jew or Jewish in a modern way?

> *Tribe (Jews often jokingly refer to themselves as Members of the Tribe)*
> *Heeb (already being used by an alternative Jewish publication, but had the right spirit)*

Obviously, this was an uphill battle. But Roger and I both really liked the word "tribe" and wanted to see where we could take it. This reminded me of a regular workshop exercise I do, in which I tell everyone that their rally cries must contain a certain word. They can decide what form, tense, or how they want to incorporate that word. In this case, we loved the word "tribe," so we began thinking and writing "tribal":

Feel the tribe
Go tribal
Join the tribe
Tribal encounter
Vibe with the tribe
Tribe members wanted
Tribal instincts

Normally, I'm used to eliciting more than twenty ideas per exercise, but since it was just the two of us, I figured that seven potential answers might do. And in fact, we used two lines from this list in our final concept.

Which ones do you think they were? Which ones would you have chosen? How would you have brought them to life?

I decided to use Join the Tribe as the tagline because to me that was the ultimate selling message. It was a broad message, it was inviting, and it said that something was going on here you might want to be a part of. I figured that the other lines could work to highlight specific programs, activities, and offerings.

Too cool for shul.

This was looking like something very fresh, very different from the Jewish organizations I remember (staid and aimed at a more traditional audience). What makes me like this concept so much is that it uses a code word that young, urban Jews really use. Also, if the focus was on dating, and making connections was the most important thing, why not just say it?

While the message of Join the Tribe was not the winning concept, Tribal Encounters was used to advertise their various dating products. It gained such popularity that is has since become the name of their next-generation dating offering.

How Different Can You Be?

Getting consumers to change their mind about your brand

With Aish, I had to deal with the all too common branding challenge of dispelling the preconceived notions. Think of all the instances where this is a challenge. When was the last time you looked forward to going to the dentist? How about getting your car inspected? Or going to a bridal shower? Just like these experiences, there are certain products, services, and industries that automatically inspire fear, uncertainty, doubt (and possibly loathing) in the minds and hearts of consumers. Buying a car typically comes with the gut feeling that you probably just got ripped off. Very few people like dealing with insurance companies, health care providers, or cell phone companies and consumers have an equally hard time relating positively to any of these kinds of companies.

That's why it's so important to explore how to overcome preconceived notions of your product, service, or brand. Think about how other breakthrough brands like Saturn got rid of the consumer belief that they were going to get ripped off in a car dealership by creating a no-haggle guarantee. Back to their tagline: "A different kind of company. A different kind of car." Progressive Insurance lets you comparison shop for insurance, even if they don't have the best prices. Their tagline? "Not what you'd expect from an insurance company." Or take Citibank, one of the largest—if not the largest—financial institutions in the world, telling you that money is not important. Breaking through the perception wall is important to explore when working with a product or service that comes with its own consumer baggage.

For the case of Aish, we wanted to create a personality that would challenge prospective members' preconceived notions of what a Jewish organization would be like. Not that Jewish organizations evoke the same feelings of dread that the dentist office does or the anxiety of an auto purchase by any means. But there were a lot of people in their target audience who were less traditional, skeptical, and more secular (including me) and a lot of us equate all-things-Jewish to our experiences as kids. Whether we were stuck in Hebrew School long after our Sunday School counterparts had been set free, or had relatives approach us at funerals and other inappropriate times wanting to fix us up with "a nice Jewish boy," what Aish needed to explore was how to sever the ties between that brand of Jewish culture and the one it wanted to portray. To do that, it had to challenge the norm.

One creative mental exercise I went through was to look back at some of the other breakthrough brands and decipher their formula for success. What it boiled down to was this question: What would you never expect this kind of company to do? You'd never expect a car dealer to give you a set price; you'd never expect an insurance company to help you get the best deal; and you'd never think your bank would tell you that money isn't important. What I needed was something that rebelled against the Jewish norm. Something that took traditional culture and turned it untraditional cool.

And here's where ideas come from anywhere in your life—your friends, your experiences, a picture you see while walking down the street. For me, I only had to think as far as my coolest Jewish friend ever. She is one of those incredibly artistic, Brooklyn-hip, alternative types who creates accessories for Old Navy by day, but whose true craft and art is handcrafted jewelry and modern Judaica (religious artifacts, gifts, or items you might find in a Jewish household). What made me think of her was her tattoo, which is forbidden by Jewish law. To make matters more interesting, her tattoo is a Star of David— the symbol of the Jewish religion. So she had gone against traditional Jewish law while using a traditional Jewish icon.

I had the visual for this concept in my mind. Now all I needed was a set of words that would bring the concept to life. Actually, I needed two sets of words—one that spoke directly to the picture at hand (the headline) and another that would become the enduring theme.

When I already have a visual thought or idea, I usually focus on creating the headline first. Sometimes the headline becomes the enduring theme in the end, but it's easier for me to start with the specific and work outward. This reminds me of an exercise that we run in workshops where we pass out a visual and simply ask them to write the perfect headline for it—whatever they think the picture conveys.

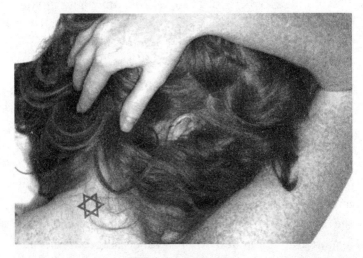

Write your headline here.

What would you do? Think about it before reading on. My answers were varied, but here are a few:

Judaism Redefined
What Is Tradition?
Surprisingly Jewish
Uncommon Wisdom

Be Your Own Jew
Look Again

I chose the line that was in the form of a question, because it's open ended. Since part of Jewish culture is questioning and debate, posing the question makes the concept less about rebellion and more about challenging perceptions and questioning the status quo. For the tagline, I decided to play it straight. I wanted to be true to the inspiration of Saturn cars and Progressive insurance and their messages. In fact, I borrowed the "not what you'd expect" from Progressive, and the "different" from Saturn and crafted those words into a tagline for Aish.

Expect something different—not the same old shtick.

In the end, I'm sorry I didn't follow the Citibank model with my rally cry. Instead of having a message focused inward on our company philosophy, Citibank spoke out to consumers and instructed them to adopt their healthy, balanced "Live Richly" financial view. Had I followed their wisdom, I definitely would have chosen the rally cry "Be your own Jew." I love that it tells people—traditional and non—that there is not one correct way to be within their faith. Then the messaging could always focus on the different kinds of members Aish attracts.

Pork Chops and Applesauce, or The "Peter Brady" Exercise
Selling the personality instead of the product

In one particularly well-known episode of *The Brady Bunch*, Peter, the middle child, is told he has no personality, so he proceeds to "try on" the personalities and voices of others, most memorably Humphrey Bogart. Once again, he was searching for an identity that he could project for others. And while he learns the lesson that he should just be himself and others will like him, today's products and brands could probably benefit from an exercise in Peter Brady branding.

Let's not confuse finding a personality with turning your product into one. One thing I can't stand is when brainstorming sessions pose the question, "If this product was a person, who would it be?" I find it to be the most insipid, idiotic question in the world. How on earth would you answer that, and why would you want to?

What would a New York City–based nonprofit organization that caters to Jewish singles be if it were a person? Let's see . . . he'd be Jewish, and live in New York City, most likely he'd be single . . . or is it she? It is infinitely harder to turn a brand into a person than it is to let that brand express itself as different people and see which one fits best. The types of personalities are endless, from the basic stereotypes (poet, jock, nerd) to the more complex creatures (tormented novelist, Eastern philosopher, accidental genius), and so the hunt for the right identity can be a lot of fun but somewhat overwhelming. Products and companies do project easily identifiable imagery. Johnson & Johnson: maternal and caring. Mountain Dew: extreme and edgy. This is entirely different from becoming a person.

We often look to people who are known for a certain style of talking and adopt their voices in order to create the right tone for our brand. For example, if you were telling someone about Aish in the voice of Humphrey Bogart, how would it come out? ("Go there and meet someone special, shweet-heart.") What about the voice of Confucius? ("Where many paths come together.") How about Rodney Dangerfield? Madonna? Betty Boop? Using others' voices is a great way to go from the idea of a brand to the expression of it.

In the case of Aish, I was hunting specifically for Jewish personalities because the Jewish personality was so important to the brand. You'll see that I didn't limit my list to just people, but included more broadly based personas as well:

Adam Sandler
A Traditional Matchmaker
The Coffee Clatch Ladies from Saturday Night Live
Moses
Typical Jewish Mother
Woody Allen
Wise Rabbi or Sage
Albert Einstein

The most important part in this or any exercise, in which you are doing an image or identity transfer, is to remember your goal. For example, Adam Sandler is known for his cleverly rhyming "Hanukkah Song" ("Let's celebrate Hanukkah/Play the harmonica/Drink a gin and tonic-ca"). Now a literal and knee-jerk reaction to using his voice might deliver such unusables as: "Aish is so fun-akkah" or "Break out your yarmulka (when you say it, it actually rhymes with Hanukkah)." The point is not to rhyme with Hanukkah, but to take what Adam Sandler did (rhyme things, talk about lesser-known Jewish celebrities, use humor) and create a rally cry or headline that evokes any or all of those things.

Can you create any? Are there others listed up there that inspire you more or whose voices are easier to imitate?

The ones that inspired me the most were the infamous nebbish, Woody Allen, and a stereotypical Jewish mother (no one said you had to choose only one). Unlike some of the other comedians, who were merely "funny Jewish men," Woody Allen is a true brand of humor. He is a character. A neurotic, self-deprecating, woman-chasing character. And Jewish mothers are just like any other mothers—they hand guilt down from generation to generation, just with New York accents. (Astute observers of ethnic culture will note that the only differences between Jewish mothers and Italian mothers are the recipes.)

I had a lot of fun imitating Woody Allen—you don't even have to be Jewish to imitate his neurotically Jewish style. Try it. How would your version of Woody Allen promote Aish NY? He might say, "Even *I* found a date there," or "It's almost too fun to be Jewish." And the Jewish mother? I almost called my own, but she's so far outside the stereotype (save the New York accent) that I spared her the effort. In the end, I ended up talking about this project with my (non-Jewish) husband that night, and it was he who summarized everything we had been trying to evoke: "All of the fun. None of the guilt."

Once he said it, I realized that this could apply to anything and everything that Aish had to offer. Now that we
had the voice we wanted, we had to make sure that the
picture reflected that same funny, quirky personality.

*If your mother
only knew
what you did
last night.*

aish
All of the fun. None of the guilt.

This personality captures the humor that's both incredibly contemporary
and inherently Jewish.

As you can see, the idea of the Jewish mother stereotype did make it back into the final iteration of the
concept. I love featuring the past generation in this
concept—there is something in it that has shades of
"Not your father's Oldsmobile" and said that the events

were truly geared to people of our—not our parents'—generation.

What's in a Name?
Turning a name into a brand

Everyone knows someone who has the curse of a bad name. Whether it's outdated (Beatrice), homonym-ly challenged (Dick), or created during a drug-drenched decade (Flower, America, or Moon Unit), your name is your moniker and can say a lot about you. Conversely, there are the Michelles, Davids, Michaels, and Jennifers who can get lost in their own ubiquity.

I once worked with a digital cable offering named MagRack. Based on that name, what would you imagine it offered? Magazine pages you could flip through with your remote? Television channels that corresponded to your magazines? Unfortunately, neither. It offered on-demand, short instructional videos and stories that focused on different activities and interests. (Who knew?)

Likewise, there are plenty of clients who have name issues. Some names seem to require foreign language lessons (I bet Au Bon Pain gets mispronounced more than The Bread Factory), others are unfortunate (Midway Airlines—who wants to get on an airline that doesn't get there "all the way"?), and still others—as was the case with Aish—with a name didn't say anything about who they were. The name was neither oddball nor omnipresent but it also didn't make much sense. In some ways, Aish was lucky—it wasn't lost among the million permutations of "J" and "Jew"-related names, such as Jdate, J2J, Single Jew, and Jcupid among others.

"Aish" literally means "fire" in Hebrew. It ignited my imagination immediately.

Fire inherently evokes so many things: passion (the fire inside), motivation (start a fire), connection (sparks fly), movement (the dancing flames), spunky (he's fiery), sexy (hottie, or hot mama)—even inspiration (spark an idea). The hardest part was trying to figure out which kind of fire would be the most motivating and appropriate one for Aish. (One point of clarification here: Aish International had been using the tagline "Igniting Jewish Pride" and, in that case, was trying to give meaning to its mysterious name. However, my goal was to bring an identity—not merely a clarification—to the name, and so my motivation was totally different.)

I wanted this concept to capture and express these inherent traits of fire. Not destructive, devilish, or hotheaded, but passionate, motivated, spunky—even sexy. When considering how "fiery" I should go, I thought back to one of my favorite William Blake quotes: "You can never know how much is enough until you've had too much." The only way to find the limits is to cross them first. In other words, don't sweat the boundaries. At least until you have to.

I had the area I wanted to work within (or push beyond), but I wasn't sure how to bring it back to the real task at hand—motivating potential members and creating an ownable brand. Looking back at my "fire" notes, I made an important correlation. Aish NY sometimes referred to itself as "Aish Connection," and "connection" was also one of the words on my list. I could smell the smoke coming out of my head as the idea started building. If it were about "sparking" connections, didn't that make them "matchmakers"? I was not so slowly becoming convinced that every single colloquialism, idiom, or cliché having to do with meeting someone, dating, or falling in love has some reference to fire. You can make a match, spark some interest, let sparks fly, and fire up a romance. You can see stars, see fireworks, start a fire, or ignite some interest. You can light up your life, kindle a romance, or fan the fires of passion. (Just hope that your romance doesn't go up in flames or flame out.) But remember, I still wanted to see how far I could go before I got burned . . . (groan).

Feel the heat: Some like it hot, but not this hot.

This concept stirred quite a few passions for the Aish team. Relating it to the *Sex and the City* characters, it was a little too "Samantha" and not enough "Charlotte." It liked that this personality gave some real fire to the Aish brand, but felt this concept went too far. Had I used some of the safer, fire-related words, maybe this concept would have been more warmly received. (Pun really not intentional there.) For me, this is a good thing because seeing what is "not you" only gives you a clearer vision of what your identity should be.

The Aish Identity
A true adventure in branding

I had had my fun. I pushed the envelope, went against the grain, explored the unexpected—even danced with the devil—but I would have been remiss if I didn't present Aish with a range of opportunities, including one that was closer in to where—and whom—it already was. I had to let Peter Brady just be Peter Brady.

So I reexamined what it was and what it offered. I thought maybe I could find a common element in all its offerings, including lectures, excursions, parties, and events. In math, we call it "finding the common denominator," and it works in branding as well.

Looking for the common brandinator is an exercise I do specifically during the pursuit of what marketers know as an "umbrella brand." True to its namesake, the umbrella brand is an overarching brand that might incorporate many different products or product platforms. For example, the umbrella brand positioning of Gatorade is sports hydration. Different products within this brand might promise more specific forms (e.g., longer-lasting hydration, instant hydration, extreme hydration), but the whole brand is about sports and hydration. One place to look for such umbrellas is in those commonalities. In this case, what do all the activities, events, and offerings of Aish NY have in common? Here is my list:

events that people do together
young singles
geared toward meeting
fun
*variety (sometimes what you have in common is
    that it's always different)*
activities

This list was okay, but there was nothing jumping out at me that sounded new, exciting, different, or inspirational. And then out of nowhere (and I mean this) a word popped into my head: Adventure. These were all adventures—social adventures, international adventures, learning adventures—the element of adventure seemed to me to be a great unifying theme, if only I could figure out how to make these *Jewish* adventures.

I knew I had to make the Jewish reference because in cases where you're creating a very broad message to a specific group of people who may not be familiar with your brand, it's important to make sure that the brand message is one that couldn't be slapped on any old product. For example, if I had just said, "Aish: The adventure awaits," you would have absolutely no clue what I was talking about without further explanation. I think that's a good rule and worth italicizing: *Between the name and the tagline, you should have a sense of what the product is and what it means to your consumer.* Again, it's a rule and therefore designed not to always be true. When is it not? For starters, when you're a huge company with a ubiquitous brand presence and a broad marketplace. It's why McDonald's can say "I'm lovin' it" (lovin' what?) or Apple can say "Think different" (different from whom?) and still work just fine.

In the case of Aish, I needed to find the word or words to put before or after "Adventure" or "Adventures" that made a reference to the Jewish nature of the organization (since that was markedly absent from its name) without saying the word "Jewish" (since that would make us sound just like everyone else). Further, a lot of young, conservative Jews will actually be turned off by something with the word "Jewish" in the name. (It often reminds me of a project we did creating a brand specifically targeted to women. Unless it's tampons or beauty products, women don't always want a brand that has the word "woman" in it, hence cereal products like Smart Start from Kellogg's and Harmony from General Mills.)

I started thinking about movie titles, but quite frankly I don't remember why. Maybe I had just walked past a movie theater or Blockbuster video store that featured an Indiana Jones DVD. Anyhow, I started imagining what I would call an adventure movie featuring Aish's events. The first line that came to my head was, "Shlomo & Marty's Most Excellent Adventure." Most awful, I know. But it did get me thinking about other movie titles, since there are plenty that contained the word "adventure." If nothing else, it might give me the right syntax or setup for the tagline. And then I realized that the trick was not to replicate the exact movie title, but to create a name that contained the same kind of excitement and action, as if it was its own movie, which eventually lead me to the tagline "Adventures in Urban Judaism." Who wouldn't rush to the box office for that flick? Once I had that much of it, the rest of the concept came easily.

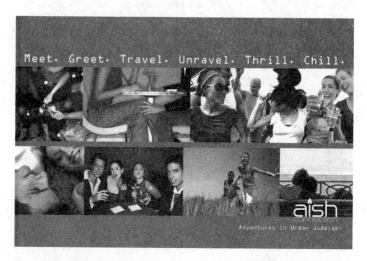

Adventures in Urban Judaism: All the elements come together.

When you think about it, any of the pictures from the past concepts could have been included in this concept, because it highlights the variety of people and offerings that Aish can provide. By design, this is not a breakthrough brand message. It pushes just far out enough to be modern and not overly religious without offending anyone.

Today, Aish NY uses its newfound identity on all of its communications—on flyers, program brochures—even on its Web site. Other branches of this association took notice, and it wasn't too long before I was asked to help all of Aish International with its brand identity and messaging. I had branded it myself in only five days, and in the process I realized I might not be such a bad Jew after all.

Build Your Own Creative Workshop

Essential warm-up exercises for the Brand-It-Yourself workout

Earlier this year, I found myself at a particularly excruciating new business pitch. Like all other new business meetings, Joe and I began to explain how our ten-day process works: "First we have the briefing, then we need a few days to create the format for the brainstorming workshops that we run. We run the brainstorming workshops with the client and with a creative team . . ." We never made it past that point because we were too busy fielding questions from the potential client who was very curious about the workshops. The client wanted to know exactly how we created the exercises: Did they come from the client briefing? Did they come from research we did? What made our techniques special? How do we take an element from the briefing and turn it into an exercise? How do we know if an idea that comes out of the workshop is a good idea?

We answered the questions the best we could, but our answers did not entirely satisfy the client. Because inherent to what he was asking is the notion that there must be a systematic process in place—a specific science that can identify and quantify opportunities together with some software program or logarithm that creates the formats for the workshops.

We tried to explain to this client that we create each format from scratch every time—every project starts out with a blank piece of paper. And while that's a seemingly archaic endeavor and totally against the grain of today's workplace tools designed for time efficiency and productivity; it's the handcrafting of each exercise that gets our creative minds in gear. This is not the only creative process out there but it is the essential beginning of ours. Creating the format warms up our brains as we begin to imagine possible solutions and opportunities.

I think my partner, Joe, did the best in describing it when he said that the exercises for the format are really half-ideas that start with many different hypotheses. Instead of developing an idea linearly, we are approaching the solution from all different angles. Those approaches are inherently creative—being creative is a problem/solution skill that makes our talents no different from any inventor who must imagine many solutions to the same problem and see which one works. It's creative because we're literally forced to imagine solutions that don't yet exist.

And this is exactly the kind of hypothesizing that we do in the workshops. Our short, one-minute exercises are hypotheses, creative guesses, mind-benders, and thought-starters that help us get real creative solutions to a wide range of challenges. There is no template, no secret formula, and no software program that we use to create the exercises. However, there are a lot of exercises that come up again and again—with variations of course. Following are some of our favorites:

1. *String theory (without the physics)*

While we always talk about single-minded ideas, sometimes the best ones come up when you put two ideas, entities, or opportunities together. To do the "string exercise," have people standing on one side of a table represent one thing, such as a specific function, concept, or benefit. On the other side is a second function, idea, or benefit (or the same one if the idea you're searching for comes from "double," i.e. Double Chocolate, Double Duty,

Double Clean). Every person on one side of the table (even if there are only two of you) is connected to a person on the other side with a piece of string. This string represents the solution—a name, a rally cry, a visual expression—and the two people together must create as many of these as possible in one minute. The two elements you put together can be complementary, such as "fast" and "easy," or "elegant" and "simple." They can be opposing, such as "tastes great" and "less filling" (sound familiar?), or "small" and "powerful." An alternate name and positioning for a small, but powerful power flosser was called MiniMax—a name that came from this very exercise.

2. *Be like Nike*

Not surprisingly, the Nike exercise works best when exploring brand ideas that seek an emotional, inspirational, or empowering identity. Pick one area to explore, from a functional claim to an inspirational message, and give participants a three-word maximum to get that message across. The Nike discipline forces brevity and taps into some very meaningful, dramatic expressions of motivation. The output from an exercise such as this can result in a great name or an even better way to communicate an emotional or inspirational brand message. There are only two rules: The rally cry you create must start with a verb and be a true call to action, such as "Reach new limits" or "Drink in life." The second is that it can't start with the word "Just" and end with the word "it."

3. *Be a rock star—or at least sing like one?*

Songwriters are poets who tap into some very powerful human emotions and their words are etched indelibly in our collective soundtrack. And that's why the "sing a song" exercise works so well. Pick one message or strategy that you want to explore, and ask participants to think of a song title or lyric that brings that thought to life. (If you leave the song exercise open-ended, the ideas will read more like a playlist on an iPod than anything else). If the strategy is "community," perhaps the Beatles' "Come Together," or the wedding favorite "We Are Family" will emerge. Either of those suggests very different brand possibilities. If the strategy is that this product fits with healthy lifestyles (as so many products are trying to convey these days), James Brown might offer the perfect first-person iteration with: "I Feel Good." People always have a better chance of winning the reward for that exercise if they sing their ideas. I remember once we did that exercise during a Weight Watchers project about how people feel after they reached their weight-loss goal. Someone blurted out, "You make me feel like dancing" (from the song "I Wanna Dance the Night Away") and gave us a brand message focused on dancing that became one of the best concepts for that project.

4. *Steal this model*

When exploring new product and loyalty opportunities for "intangible" products such as auto insurance policies, magazine subscriptions, or other membership programs, look to other membership and services companies for ideas. Think about discount clubs at supermarkets and bookstores, prepaid phone and gift cards, loyalty programs at hotels, drugstores, gas stations. These kinds of lucrative business ideas can be applied and adapted ad infinitum. It was this exercise that inspired a lot of our thinking in the toughest membership challenge to date—book clubs. We needed to create profitable plans that get away from those typical offers that include taping a penny to the reply card, which then commits you to two years of "negative option" buying. The Sam's Club model gave us a membership card that allowed deeply discounted prices on all books purchased, we modeled a subscription plan after magazines, and used prepaid phone cards and gift cards as inspiration for a prepaid book card. The same exercise works as well for packaged goods. You can use this when examining packaging configurations and innovations, pricing offers and promotional ideas.

5. *Play "What If?"*

There is something magical about the words "What if . . ." It plays into your deepest fantasies. It essentially allows people to create the ideal product, service, brand, or communication without feeling like their ideas have to be grounded in reality. Let people just blurt out as many What Ifs as they can in two minutes. (Setting a time limit will keep this exercise under control.) After the two minutes are up, give everyone one minute to take one of the blue-sky ideas and create an idea that brings it back to Earth with a more realistic product or a more viable promise. If the initial idea was a product (and this one always comes up for some reason) in a self-heating or self-cooling can, the realistic application might simply be an insulated package that keeps the beverage hotter longer or cooler longer, or even a minty or spicy flavor. In the pharmaceutical industry and other industries that are very limited by what they can say or claim, this is a good mental exercise that pushes thinking out before having to reign it in. Tapping into people's imaginations is what What If is all about.

6. *Think visual*

As I've mentioned before, thinking visual is an amazing way to create and capture meaningful brand ideas, and it's so essential to any workshop format that it's worth risking redundancy to include it here. Billboards, snapshots, paintings, icons—any canvas is going to be a winning source of new and fresh ideas. Maybe a picture is worth a thousand words, but, more important, it brings out ideas that words do not always convey. The best way to craft this exercise is to make sure that the visual of choice has one of two restrictions: First, you give people one specific benefit, emotion, function, or promise that forces them to focus their visual thinking; or second, the image must be a still image, not a moving one. This keeps people from wandering into the before and after of the message when all you're looking for is the real meat of the idea. Once the visual thinking is complete, words can reenter the picture in the form of painting titles, photo captions, or the one great word that captures the sentiment of the visual. These usually end up being the best names and rally cries of an entire session.

7. *From exaggeration to eureka*

This exercise requires participants to give a demonstration of efficacy in a less-than-expected way. The exercise starts out: This product is so [*insert promise here: fast, easy, effective, delicious, etc.*], that. . . . Let people fill in the blanks and, more often than not, you'll find yourself with some less-than-likely demonstrations, which are precisely the ones you want. Think about what Palmolive did with a dishwashing liquid so gentle on hands that you would actually find it at the nail salon. By hunting for the exaggerated expression, you can make an extraordinary brand promise. We once used this exercise with a toothbrush that could help remove stains from teeth. The answer we got was that it "removed stains so well, that *people polish their china with it*." That inspired a great demonstration where the brush removed coffee stains from a cup, which everyone relates to and which is much nicer than showing it removing coffee stains from teeth.

8. *Please try this at home*

Give someone a test, and they'll take it. Tie that to the need for your product and you've got the beginnings of a great idea. The Kellogg's Special K cereal test encouraged people to see if they could "pinch an inch" on their waistlines. If they could (who couldn't?) they needed to start eating Special K. The demonstration exercise is undoubtedly one of the most difficult exercises you can do in a workshop setting, and often one of the most rewarding. Like all the other exercises, you want to ground the demonstration in something specific and let participants create around that one function or benefit (demonstrations typically surround functional claims). In a project whose goal was to boost the popularity of wet cat food, we asked participants to create a demonstration about its total taste appeal. The test we created was a taste test between wet and dry cat food: Place a bowl of each in front of your cat, and see which one it goes to first. We all know the outcome of this test, and yet it serves as a great motivater to cat owners who, more than anything, want to keep their pets happy. It's one thing to know that a product works, but it's entirely different when you can prove it.

9. *Where in the world . . .*

It's the oldest trick in the book and I hate to admit that it still works. From California Pizza Kitchen and Hawaiian Tropic suntan lotion, to Russian vodka and British gin, the right location is everything. You can get a group of people hunting for the perfect geographical imagery using something as simple as an airline ticket jacket or a blank postcard. Hand out these items and ask people to tell us where in the world they were when they discovered this new product. If it's a food or beverage, flavors can be explored. Health and beauty products are also renown for this kind of evocative imagery. The place can be large ("the East"), regional ("Southwest"), local ("East Hampton"), even invented ("The Secret Garden"). In the workshops, it's great to allow participants to go wherever they want and enjoy wherever it is their imagination takes them.

10. *Put their wine in your mouth*

This has got to be one of the most productive exercises of all time. Have the group blurt out a list of one of the following: their favorite brands outside their category (Fed-Ex, Apple, and BMW always surface), philosophers and thought leaders (Confucius and George Washington are popular), or great personalities (Woody Allen, George Carlin, and Marilyn Monroe top my list). Once they've done that, give everyone a minute to create a tagline, rally cry, or selling message using the voice of that person or brand. Each brand or persona can inspire an entirely unique product personality or selling message. George Washington is truthful, honest; George Carlin is good at crafting lofty descriptors. FedEx guarantees service and delivery, while BMW provides ultimate performance. By matching your product with successful brand promises and personalities, you can really open up the possibilities.

Please bear in mind that there is no hard and fast rule for creating exercises. You start with a strategy, a benefit, an emotion you want to explore, and then craft the exercise to help elicit creative solutions. It's all about getting people to approach challenges from a new direction and then express their ideas in a new way. Chances are, you're already thinking of a few of your own exercises already. You don't need a large group to do the exercises, although in my opinion the more minds you have, the more ideas you create. In fact, you can even create the exercises and then complete them by yourself. It might not be as much fun as doing it with a group of people, but I guarantee that you will still unearth some language, ideas, and visual thoughts that can lead you to a great brand solution.

Back to those questions from that client meeting: How do we know that we haven't missed an idea? Or that a great idea was overlooked? We never know for sure. There are plenty of new products, new services, brands, or repositionings that are brilliant. Some such as Red Bull, Dove, Citigroup, and iPod I wish I had done myself.

In the end, the doubtful client didn't hire us, even though we had already completed numerous successful projects with his company. And that's okay. One client at Coca-Cola, for whom I have great respect, once said to me, "There are many ways to develop a brand and many approaches to that end. You guys are just one of those ways." If we had a formula that unconditionally guaranteed marketplace success with each project, we'd probably charge a whole lot more than we do now. I approach branding and developing the brand character creatively. Others approach it strategically. No matter which approach you choose, branding is a process and needs to be approached step-by-step. Brands were not built in a day. Conversely, they shouldn't take forever.

Avoid the Quagmires

Mistakes and missteps based on firsthand experience

If we had no faults we should not take so much pleasure in pointing out the faults of others.

—*François De La Rochefoucauld*

I have had my fair share of bad ideas. There have been concepts (and products, and names, and taglines) that when I look back on them I can't decide whether I should destroy all the evidence, or wear them as my personal albatross. One of the beauties of creating nearly twenty ideas per project, is that it gives you some room for error. While you don't have to match my output (even I couldn't get to twenty when doing it on my own), it's a good idea in your own work to give yourself some conceptual wiggle room and have a number in your head of the amount of branding concepts you would like to create. Having a specific number in mind acts as both an inspirational goal ("Only two more left!") and disciplinary ("Is this concept-worthy?"). I recommend somewhere between five and ten concepts. Within the spectrum of ideas, it's not unlikely that there's a real loser in the bunch, although we never know what it is until it comes out. That is, except for one particularly ill-fated project that contained a disproportionate amount of some of the most awful ideas we've ever spawned.

We were supposed to create new brands of cereal for Post; sweetened flakes (oat, corn, or wheat) that would appeal to both grown-ups and their kids. The concepts were full of corny names, like "King of Crunch" and "Mt. Crunchmore" and contained some of the least appealing imagery, with brands like "Firehouse Flakes" (made from the dandruff of firefighters?) or "Cowboy Crisps" (what the Marlboro man eats for breakfast). While a few good ideas made it into the fray, it reminds me that becoming a great brandmaker is just as much about where you *don't* go as where you do.

In looking back at our own best-efforts-gone-bad, I can see that many of the missteps happened in similar places. Like anything else, there are patterns. I'd like to couple my own less-than-perfect moments with a few re-curring ones of the client side of the equation. While I don't believe that any of these will spell disaster for your brand, avoiding these common—and sometimes costly—pitfalls will save you a lot of time and angst.

1. *No pun in-ten-did (well)*

As much as I enjoy puns in my personal life, I avoid in-cluding them in any concept I write. Double entendres al-ways come up in workshops and people constantly pat themselves on the back for their cleverness and "double meaning." These kinds of names and rally cries are easily recognizable because they usually end with the words, "Get it?" But just because something is clever, doesn't mean it's good. Remember that most puns are lousy—that's why they make people groan, and that is not the re-action you want to evoke with your product. If a pun is actually clever, it's going to fly over the heads of most folks, and that's not good either. We once created a con-cept for a fast-food restaurant that said their new chicken sandwich was so value priced, it was "nothing to 'bawk' at." What were we thinking? Puns and mass marketing just don't work. Puns and non–mass marketing also don't work. Or as they'd say on *Cops*:

"Step . . . away . . . from . . . the . . . puns."

2. *No negatives*

Except in politics, negative campaigning breeds negative results. While people feel very strongly about not voting for a shady politician, the same emotions are not in play when buying groceries. It's like that old saw that says when you say something bad about a person the bad vibe somehow sticks to you. I have made these kinds of comparisons (with client consent) again and again and not once in over three hundred projects has that concept become the winning idea. It's never even made it to the top five. Furthermore, creating the negative sets the rivalry between brands. Coke vs. Pepsi, Lays vs. Pringles, Bud Lite vs. Miller Lite. Think about when you eat dinner with a bickering couple with each one vying for the title of The One That's in the Right. Unless you do it with extreme care and cleverness, it's likely to become a corporate version of the Hatfields and the McCoys, and it's uncomfortable for everyone.

3. *Don't focus only on problem areas*

I have had more than my fair share of concepts that start by identifying a problem that the product in question is designed to eliminate. This setup stems from the very smart theory that the more you set up the problem, the better the solution sounds. However, when showing an idea that only highlights the problem, it is an instant turnoff for consumers. Back to that failure of a cereal project . . . we had a concept that solved the problem of soggy cereal because of a special sugar coating on the flakes that could actually help keep the cereal crunchier longer in milk. So we communicated this idea with a picture of a kid frowning, holding up a spoon with a limp flake hanging off it. This was so unappealing, it evoked pity at best and indelibly associated that sad cereal experience with our brand. Had we identified the soggy scene with another brand, and balanced the negative image with a positive one of a happy kid crunching along, maybe this would have worked. Or if we were really smart, maybe we'd have just shown the second picture, the positive experience that comes from never having soggy cereal. Positive messaging and imagery nearly always brings in more positive results—from our clients and from consumers themselves.

4. *Don't wear your price tag on your sleeve*

Placing your whole brand message on one price point can get tricky. During the Internet heyday, we worked with a commercial real estate company that took only 40 percent of the typical broker's commission and applied the rest to pay for the tenant's first month of rent. While this is a real enticement, it would have been a huge mistake to end branding message there. If the whole message revolved around this one free month, it would only be a matter of time before the competition offered two free months, and put it out of business. It's one thing to guarantee value and discount, and another to guarantee a certain price point. If you own the All-for-a-Dollar chain of stores, it's only a matter of time before someone parks their 99-cent store right next door.

5. *The doctor is no longer "in"*

Can you tell me the number-one Doctor Recommended brand of analgesic? Cough syrup? Decongestant? Nasal spray? There are so many doctor recommendations out there that the message has lost its power. What's more, consumers have wised up to the fact that most doctor recommendations and usage claims (e.g., "Tylenol is the brand used most in hospitals") are earned by giving out a lot of free samples or even more free dinners to the medical profession. Experts proclaiming nirvana on products and services—while still immensely popular—is a tired way of marketing. You're better off making up a new recommender. These give you more room for creative and unique endorsements, such as the "Dental Experts" at Oral B (who are those guys?) or the "Ponds Institute," which is nothing more than a sign posted on an empty door. In fact, while this book is not the number-one Doctor Recommended Book on Branding, it is a book endorsed by the Branding Professionals of America (BPA), the New Product Marketing Alliance (NPMA), and the Fast Branders of America (FBA). Well, it would be if any of them really existed.

6. *Imitation is the worst kind of branding*

In new product invention, there's a tendency to see a marketplace trend and back-fit your brand into it. By the time your product has launched, the trend is already over. How many low-carb entries into the grocery store are still around? How many SUVs are there in the world all fighting for the same market share while demand for a Prius is higher than ever? Why not spend the same time and money on innovation and not imitation? When iMacs came out and challenged the beige-PC norm, it was only a matter of months before PC computers followed suit. And just like in the world of fashion, creating the knockoff just makes the original that much more coveted. (Do you pay less for a real Louis Vuitton bag just because you can get a fake one for twenty bucks on the street corner? I don't think so.) Taking an idea that is successful and slapping it on your product is just not good competition. How much better would it have been if Dell or Gateway had used iMac to inspire them to create different-looking computers, but created a new look instead of copying Apple?

They could have ones that evoked the brushed steel so popular in kitchens, or ones with animal prints, or ones designed by fashion and home gurus (who wouldn't want the Todd Oldham PC?). Instead, they put their boring beige towers into not-that-stylish iMac rip offs. When that didn't work, they decided to retreat to one color. But it wasn't a total loss. Now instead of them all being beige, some are also black.

7. Don't look back

In a campaign speech early in his career, Franklin D. Roosevelt said: "Competition has been shown to be useful up to a certain point and no further." FDR raises an interesting issue when you examine this quote in marketing terms. Are competitive claims useful only up to a certain point? We are no strangers to the competitive claim. It is a clear and logical way to demonstrate to consumers why and how you are different from those in your competitive set. Here's the problem with them (or a lot of functional claims) on their own: You leave yourself vulnerable for someone to come and beat you at your own claim. If you can outdo your competition on speed, efficacy, or price, you don't need a Magic 8-Ball to tell you that your competition can and will come out with claims that are just as good—if not better—than yours.

The leader in any category will never make a competitive claim, because it doesn't have to. Once you set your sights on another product, you instantly admit that they are the ones to beat. And what happens once you outdo them? Then what is your brand about? This is the "certain point and no further" that FDR may have been making had he been talking about marketing and not the New Deal.

8. *Don't forget your native language*

When I write a letter to customer service or my building's management company, I take on this very proper and haughty, self-important tone. Instead of saying that I saw a mistake on my bill, I'll say, "It has come to my attention that an error has been made while processing my last payment invoice." While I think it makes me sound smarter and more authoritative, what it's really doing is making me sound kind of silly. I see a similarly strange phenomenon in marketing land in concept writing: Incredibly intelligent marketers, graduates of top business schools, veterans of consumer insights and learning have forgotten how to write in simple English. I have seen concepts they have written that contain ridiculous phrases like "scrumptiously deliciously delicious" or far-fetched, questionable insights, such as "There are some times when you crave a snack that is meaty *and* crunchy at the same time." Or else the syntax sounds incredibly awkward: "Introducing the cleaning product that is sure to make a great addition to your household because of its super cleaning agents and fresh scent that make it a delight." (Huh?) Financial and technological companies also get lost in their own jargon to the point that their concepts usually require a translator, or at least a dictionary of terms. When writing a concept, write it the way you'd explain it to a friend, using simple everyday language that real people use.

9. *Don't borrow interest unless you're going to pay it off*

One of the lessons hardest for me to learn was the notion of "borrowed interest." Even after being told several times not to borrow interest, I don't think I even understood what it means. Until Firehouse Flakes came along, that is. In this concept we borrowed heroism and imagery that had absolutely nothing to do with our product whatsoever. I made matters even worse by trying to make that link: Firefighters need to eat a good breakfast . . . we are that good breakfast . . . and so we are from the firehouse. It would have been much smarter had we branded them "Hearty Flakes," "Good Morning Cereal," or anything else that then would have made the firefighter story more believable. But no, we got greedy and paid the price with an idea that was killed before it even took its first breath.

10. *F**k the box*

In writing this book, my editor was dismayed more than once about the amount of clichés I used in my writing. I told him that I was going to quit using clichés cold turkey, until I realized I was doing what I am so quick to judge in others who use clichés in order to tell people that you plan on not using clichés. The best way to think "outside the box" is to forget that the box exists at all. Phrases I have heard more than one hundred times in workshops and meetings include: "24/7" (yes, that goes for 25/8 as well), "pushing the envelope," "Pinnacle," "Apex," "Compass" (those last three are big with financial companies), and "Anything 2k." (Millennium's over, folks, or as a cliché expert would say, "It's so last year.") What's worse is when people are so determined to "think outside the box" that they totally lose their minds. Often, it's industry jargon for wanting to do something outrageous or other times it's a transparent excuse to do silly, frivolous advertising. Some people will heroically claim that "risk is its own reward," which is a pretty stupid theory when you think about it. I like to say that risk is its own risk, and every once in a while you might get rewarded for it. There have been plenty of risky ideas that have been a huge flop. The first that comes to mind is those mutant gerbils for Quiznos. Granted, it's a very nontraditional idea to use rodents as

spokespeople for food and it definitely sells their sand-
wiches on something besides the cold cut combinations.
But unfortunately, it's also totally disgusting. And while
hindsight is always just that, when pushing into some
farther-out ideas, it's a good idea to avoid nauseating your
audience (unless, of course, your product is Ipecac syrup,
then go right ahead).

It caused a stir, just not the right one.

The point is, that there's a way to accomplish all that
"going against the grain," "thinking out of the box," and
"pushing the envelope" kind of branding without going
totally bonkers. By the same token, if you know about
slang, hipster words such as "Phat" or "Bling," chances are
they're no longer dope with the crowd you're to reach.

We just hired a new assistant art director and we had

asked her to create a rendering of a new toothbrush for kids. We had told her that the design should look like a giraffe, meaning that the handle and neck might have a design similar to a giraffe print. After working on it for a few hours, she confronted our senior art director with what she had done:

Very cute, but very wrong.

Of course, this wasn't what we had in mind (although it was darn cute) and we all got a good laugh from her misinterpretation. While a lot of people might have been embarrassed and thrown their mistake in the trash, instead this art director announced: "I'm going to create a Bloopers folder and have this be the first entry." I think all of us should have a Bloopers folder where we can admit our mistakes, have a good laugh, and maybe even make some more.

Making fewer mistakes comes only with practice (and some good guidelines, of course), but to avoid all errors completely would take half the fun out of being creative. In my family, we have a philosophy about telling jokes: They're not all good, but you've got to get them out there. It's the same in any creative endeavor. The missteps and mistakes are part of the process that lets you get bad ideas out of the way for better ones to come through. I'm sure that there are many more really bad concepts I've come up with that have flaws besides the ones I've mentioned, and I'd like to take this opportunity to tell any of my clients who might have endured one of these concepts: Sorry about that.

Branding Faster into the Future

The ever-quickening race to the marketplace

Branding reminds me of Madonna. No matter what decade it is, she maintains her star quality by evolving to match the fashion of the day. Similarly, branding has fallen subject to its own popularity, and what defines a brand has changed with the marketplace. Back in the day, a brand was just considered your logo or name. Focus groups were not a million-dollar industry, new products were technology-driven, and the idea of branding anything based on pure emotion would have seemed absurd. And yet here we find ourselves in a world of advanced-stage branding, with more than seven hundred brands of water, seven thousand brands of credit cards, and seven million books on branding. Today, branding is the ultimate catchword that covers everything from the imagery you evoke to the purpose you provide. For some, it's about owning a certain visual cue (the ubiquitously white iPod headphones), for others, it's a demonstration of functionality (Bounty, the Quicker Picker-Upper). And, for still others, it is an emotional relationship, a badge, a set of words, a sentiment, a philosophy, a reaction, a club, an adjective, a piece of poetry, or a style that defines and distinguishes a brand.

If this is how things look today, what will the future hold? Is society—and shelf space—going to become simpler, or that much more saturated? Will it be Gillette or Schick that will out-blade the other? Who will be the first to introduce the ten-blade razor or will one of them resurrect the straight razor as the new simplicity of shaving? And how would you brand either one of those?

As brands—and branding as an industry—moves into the future, companies and the marketers within them need to become even more flexible, agile, and ultimately, timely in the way they approach such endeavors. Making a brand stand out in the marketplace will get more challenging; and, if history is any indication, companies will be forced to speed up the process even more. Gone will be the days when companies have the luxury of having a "standardized process" for creating, testing, and launching new products. Besides, standardized processes produce standard ideas, and frankly that's just not going to cut it. Already we've seen what happens when a product like Red Bull cuts through the marketplace and forces big companies to bob in their wakes, mouths agape before they rush to follow in their footsteps. Look on the shelves today and nearly every major beverage company (and lots of minor ones) offers their own version of a Red Bull without one fraction of the success.

Or when it comes to being a trend follower and not a trend leader, all you have to do is look at the low-carb phenomenon. If you went inside a supermarket during the year 2004, you couldn't ignore the rash of Atkins-friendly products that appeared, seemingly out of nowhere. Within the course of just a month or two, products loaded with protein, fat, and sugar alcohols sprouted in every category—ice creams, cereals, yogurts, chocolate bars, breads (low-carb bread? that's like low-fat lard!). You name it, they made it, and nearly every offering tasted absolutely revolting. And then as quickly as they came, they were gone. Consumers decided that the all-protein, low-carb, taste-free lifestyle was no longer for them. What companies were left with was a corporate Spruce Goose with an enormous price tag to match.

The lesson to be learned is something that's staring most marketers in the face: From home equity loans to frozen side dishes, consumers are feeling simultaneously more overloaded with information and more time constrained than ever. Never before have I worked on so many products designed to help people deal with their "busy lifestyles": effortless credit-card rewards, gourmet frozen foods, meal replacement bars. Simultaneously, marketers themselves are feeling busier than ever, churning out more new products and having less time to get them there. No wonder marketers find themselves practically tripping over themselves and one another in order to get new products and brands onto the shelves, each racing toward success. Delta introduced its budget Song Airlines with the inspiration of jetBlue and the intention that if it didn't work within a year, it would be scrapped. (It hasn't yet, but hope springs eternal.) As we continue in this direction, it becomes cheaper and easier to produce a product and get it out there than to risk having someone else beat you to it. In the battle over shelf space and wallet space, it looks like timing really is everything.

This is nothing new to us and to the appeal of our business model. In the early days of our business, companies hired us because we were quick and cheap, and we came off as a low-risk experiment. A few years later, the explosion of the Internet, the entrepreneurial mind-set (not to mention the truckloads of venture capital), and the race to create a profitable e-biz with a domain name not-yet-taken made our quick turnaround time and creative approach right in line with the mind-set of the environment. And when all the venture capital was gone and the economy was taking a dive, our quick-and-cheap angle made a comeback. What we see now and for the future is very different than in the past: People are hiring us for one thing and one thing only—speed. Our quick turn-around and ten-day discipline has proven invaluable to companies who, within a few weeks, can get meaningful ideas that actually shortcut their entire market research process and get them one step closer to the marketplace.

On the other side of the time it takes to create ideas is the time it takes to make judgments on them and decide which ones to move ahead on. Did Thomas Edison use a focus group to make sure the light bulb would sell? Would he do so today? And would it test well? It sounds like a silly question, but think about it.

Can we put a product on the shelves without testing it to death?

The expense of creating and maintaining successful products and brands has become a pricey venture for most big companies. It stands to reason that the marketers within these companies want to make sure that con-sumers will consume enough of a certain brand to make all the manufacturing and marketing worthwhile. Which gives consumers a lot of shareholder power in the success or failure of any brand-building effort. After spending many weeks, months, even years focusing on what the target audience wants, clients become caught up in how badly they need the consumer to want whatever it is they're selling. It's the classic case of Desperate Lover Syndrome—the more approval you seek, the harder it is to obtain. And, frankly, whatever you're selling becomes less attractive.

It reminds me of a project we were working on with Pharmavite, admittedly one of my favorite clients, on its Nature Made vitamins brand. Our task was to come out with new lines of vitamins and new offerings. Partner-ships, co-branding, and new forms and packaging were all on the table as viable opportunity avenues. If you take a look at the Nature Made shelf, you will see rows of bland brown bottles with yellow labels lined up in alphabetical order with the name of the active ingredient prominently placed. Acidophilus...Alpha Lipoic Acid...Antioxidant Pack...Beta Carotene...Calcium Magnesium...Chromium Picolinate...CoQ10...and so on.

In creating a new line of vitamins, one thing we wanted to explore was talking about benefits in a new way, or talking about active ingredients in a new way. For example, fish oil is a very hot ingredient right now for its heart-healthy benefits. But there is no obvious answer to what makes one brand's fish oil different from the next. Maybe one is coated not to give you "fish burps," in industry-speak. But that's a technological advancement, not a branding advancement, and one that can be readily imitated by any other company. So, instead, we proposed a line of vitamins based on healthy diets from around the world, with one variety being the Mediterranean diet, being high in fish oil, lycopene, and other heart-healthy ingredients. The client let us proceed with this idea, but he was more excited about another product that added an energy component to an existing bone and joint supplement they offered. As marketers, we said, "Well, why don't we give the energy one a little personality or even inspiration—maybe we could create a Nike-esque version of the product so there would be the regular SKU and the one 'for the sport.'" Perhaps this would be the first time ever that glucosamine might not seem so geriatric. However, the client said, "Well, I would prefer if you just talked about it as joint health *plus energy*. Maybe I've listened to too many consumers talk about energy, but I think it's what they really want." (And what will happen five years from now? What will be the new trend? Trans-fatty this or that. Eat this food and your cholesterol will lower fifty points. Alpha Lipoic Acid becomes the holy grail of longevity. How far ahead of the trend should you be? Too far out and nobody takes it seriously—they laugh. Not far out enough, and you're dull, lost among a sea of parity.)

I keep waiting for the real visionaries to come along and say, "This is a good idea. I want to be the first. I'm willing to take some chances." Those days are long gone, I fear. So far gone that I'm happy with the fact that people will push out far enough to at least consider some of those chancier ideas of ours for even a minute before they kill them and take the safe route.

Still, you have to keep creating, don't you?

Again and again, it serves as a reminder that loving an idea you created is far better than falling in love with it. You've heard the phrase, "I like that idea, but I'm not married to it," and that's how I relate to my branding and new product creations. Being married to an idea is being totally unaware that there may be faults and flaws. It's a mistake for anyone to believe that he or she alone holds such great powers of judgment and authority. (Some genius at RCA decided that Dimensia was the perfect name for a line of home-theater products.)

When clients don't like a particular concept, they don't have to justify it. They can just not like it. I, on the other hand, am asked to explain why I think it works. But then if I have to explain it too much, why bother? I have made great pleas for ideas I believed were worth fighting for when the client didn't grasp the heart, soul, and utter brilliance of what I believed to be something very original and effective. Other times, it's better to nod in agreement and support their choices because they may have certain corporate imperatives and information I'm not privy to. Ultimately, they make the decisions, not I.

In your case, you may want to show your brand ideas to coworkers, potential customers, even friendly marketers, although I recommend *selling* your idea instead of *asking* for approval. The more finished you can make it look, feel, or sound, the better. Cut out pictures from magazines, look at online stock photography houses, mock up a label because the less other people have to work to see your vision the better off you are.

When it comes to Branding It Yourself, there will always be a future in ideas, no matter how fast you have to deliver them. Teaching you how to create your own ideas does not lessen the value of the ones I create.

The best ideas happen when we realize that ideas are a commodity. There's no limit to how many you can create. It's all in how you develop them, massage them, bring them to life. It's about letting others improve on the ideas we begin with, letting their expertise start where ours ends and ultimately letting go of the belief that only one brand idea can be the right one—which may be the hardest thing any of us can learn to do.

Acknowledgments

Appreciation is a wonderful thing: It makes what is excellent
in others belong to us as well.

—*Voltaire*

Special thanks to my partner Joe Viverito and our team of
fearless Brandmakers: Gingi Tilbury, Karen Sabal, Sarah
Schoenberg, Deborah Magocsi, Caroline Wallace, and
Merrill Feitell.

Thanks to the clients who let their stories be told:
Michele Jaworski, Chris Edwards, Rabbi Adam Jacobs,
and Team DQ: Aric Nissen, Michael Keller, Mike Rinke,
and Dean Peters.

To Laureen Rowland and Doug Garr who were instru-
mental in making this book a reality.

Lastly, I'd like to thank my parents, Renee and Ted, my
brother Richard, and my husband Gus for all their love
and support.

The following photographs appear courtesy of Getty Images: